BLACK&DECKER®
HOME IMPROVEMENT LIBRARY™

Workshop
Tips & Techniques

Cy DeCosse Incorporated
Minnetonka, Minnesota

Contents

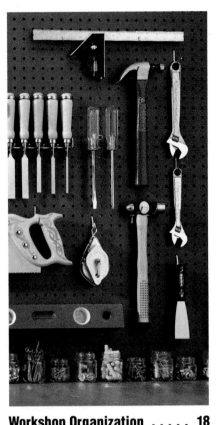

Copyright © 1991
Cy DeCosse Incorporated
5900 Green Oak Drive
Minnetonka, Minnesota 55343
1-800-328-3895
All rights reserved
Printed in U.S.A.

Also available from the publisher:
*Everyday Home Repairs, Decorating with
Paint & Wallcovering, Carpentry: Tools •
Shelves • Walls • Doors, Kitchen
Remodeling, Building Decks, Home
Plumbing Projects & Repairs, Basic
Wiring & Electrical Repairs*

Library of Congress
Cataloging-in-Publication Data

Workshop tips & techniques

p. cm.— (Black & Decker home
improvement library)
Includes index.
ISBN 0-86573-716-9.
ISBN 0-86573-717-7 (pbk.)
1. Workshops.
I. Cy DeCosse Incorporated
II. Title: Workshop tips and techniques.
III. Series.
TT152.W68 1991   90-28783
684'.08—dc20

CY DECOSSE INCORPORATED
Chairman: Cy DeCosse
President: James B. Maus
Executive Vice President: William B. Jones

Created by: The Editors of Cy DeCosse
Incorporated, in cooperation with Black &
Decker. **BLACK&DECKER** is a trademark
of the Black & Decker Corporation, and is
used under license.

Managing Editor: Paul Currie
Editor: Bryan Trandem
Project Manager: Dianne Talmage
Senior Art Director: Tim Himsel
Copy Editors: Janice Cauley,
  Bernie Maehren
Art Director: Dave Schelitzche
Director of Development, Planning &
  Production: Jim Bindas
Production Manager: Amelia Merz
Shop Supervisor: Greg Wallace
Prop Stylist & Researcher: Jim Huntley
Photo Director: Christopher Wilson

Electronic Publishing Analyst:
  Kevin D. Frakes
Production Staff: Joe Fahey, Melissa
  Grabanski, Mark Jacobson, Yelena
  Konrardy, Daniel Meyers, Linda
  Schloegel, Nik Wogstad

Studio Manager: Rebecca Boyle

Photographers: Phil Aarestad, Rudy Calin,
  Paul Englund, Rex Irmen, John Lauenstein,
  Mark Macemon, Chuck Nields, Mette
  Nielsen, Mike Parker, Cathleen Shannon,
  Hugh Sherwood

Contributing Writers & Editors: John Riha,
  Greg Breining

Contributing Manufacturers: Armstrong
  World Industries, Inc.; Cooper Industries;
  Sonin Inc.; Waxman Industries, Inc.;
  Wedge Innovations

Color Separations: Hong Kong Scanner
  Craft Co. Ltd.
Printing: R. R. Donnelley & Sons (0791)

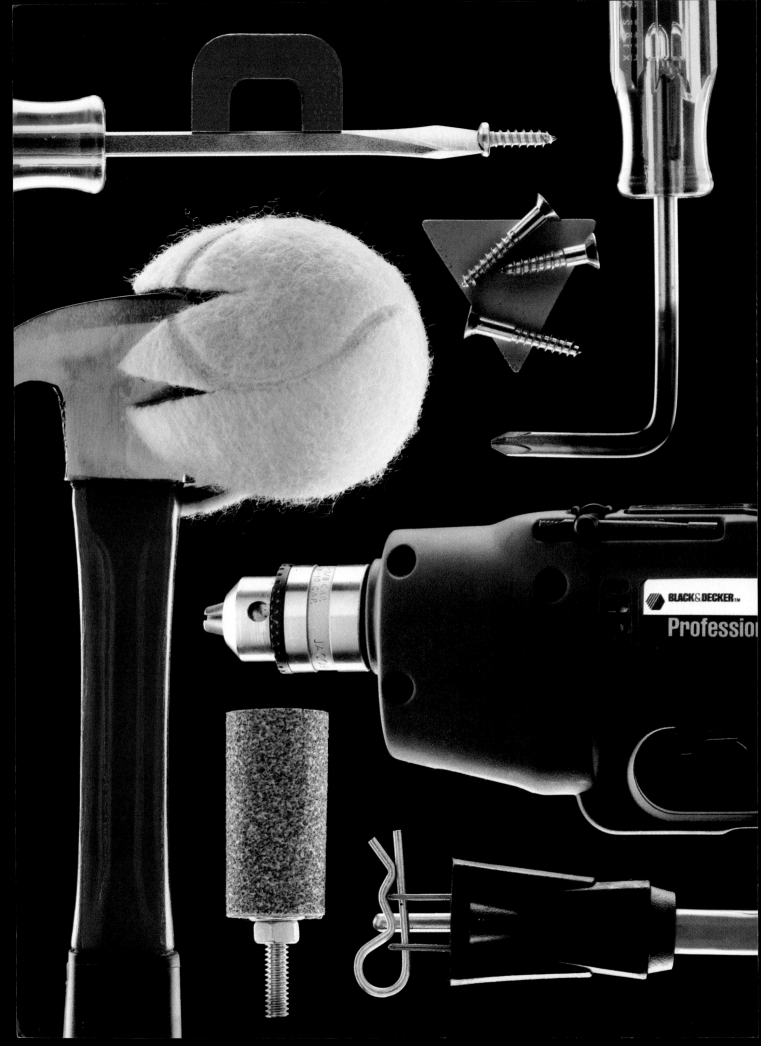

Introduction

Workshop Tips & Techniques is designed to help you get the most from your workshop and the work you do there. Whether you are a novice do-it-yourselfer or an advanced woodworker, you will find many helpful ideas in this book. More than 500 photographs illustrate tips and techniques gathered by hobbyists, woodworkers, and professional builders over years of working with workshop and construction materials. These tips and techniques, covering all aspects of workshop planning, tool use, and project craftsmanship, will save you time and money.

The first section, "Workshop Basics," will show you how to make your workshop a safe place in which to work. You learn how to set up lights to best illuminate the work area, and how to provide adequate electrical service for the shop. A number of methods for soundproofing and ventilating the workshop are presented here. This section also shows you safe and easy ways to get materials from the lumberyard and into the shop.

"Workshop Organization" contains many ideas to help you organize your tools and materials and make the best use of valuable work space. Plus, we give you simple plans and how-to steps for building three helpful storage projects.

The next chapter, "Tools," helps you care for and get more accurate results from the hand and power tools in your workshop. It demonstrates techniques that professionals use with their tools. We also show you how to make a variety of specialty tools out of old, worn-out

tools. Construction sequences are provided for making cutting guides and tool accessories.

"Workshop Techniques" guides you through many methods for improving your project skills. Tips for measuring, making patterns, using clamps and adhesives, sanding, and finishing and painting will make your work quicker and easier, and your projects more attractive.

Keeping your shop area clean, recycling shop materials, and using leftover household items as shop aids are the subjects of the last section, "Workshop Cleanup and Recycling." This section also shows you methods for safely disposing of hazardous waste materials.

A clean, well-organized workshop and the fine projects you create there can provide a great sense of satisfaction. *Workshop Tips & Techniques* will help you achieve that satisfaction safely, inexpensively, and efficiently.

Do you have a favorite tip from your workshop experience that you would like to share with others? We may be able to use it in an upcoming book. If you would like to do so, send it to us:

The Editors
Black & Decker® Home Improvement Library™
5900 Green Oak Drive
Minnetonka, Minnesota 55343

NOTICE TO READERS

This book provides useful instructions, but we cannot anticipate all of your working conditions or the characteristics of your materials and tools. For safety, you should use caution, care, and good judgment when following the procedures described in this book. Consider your own skill level and the instructions and safety precautions associated with the various tools and materials shown. Neither the publisher nor Black & Decker® can assume responsibility for any damage to property or injury to persons as a result of misuse of the information provided.

The instructions in this book conform to "The Uniform Plumbing Code," "The National Electrical Code Reference Book," and "The Uniform Building Code" current at the time of its original publication. Consult your local Building Department for information on building permits, codes, and other laws as they apply to your project.

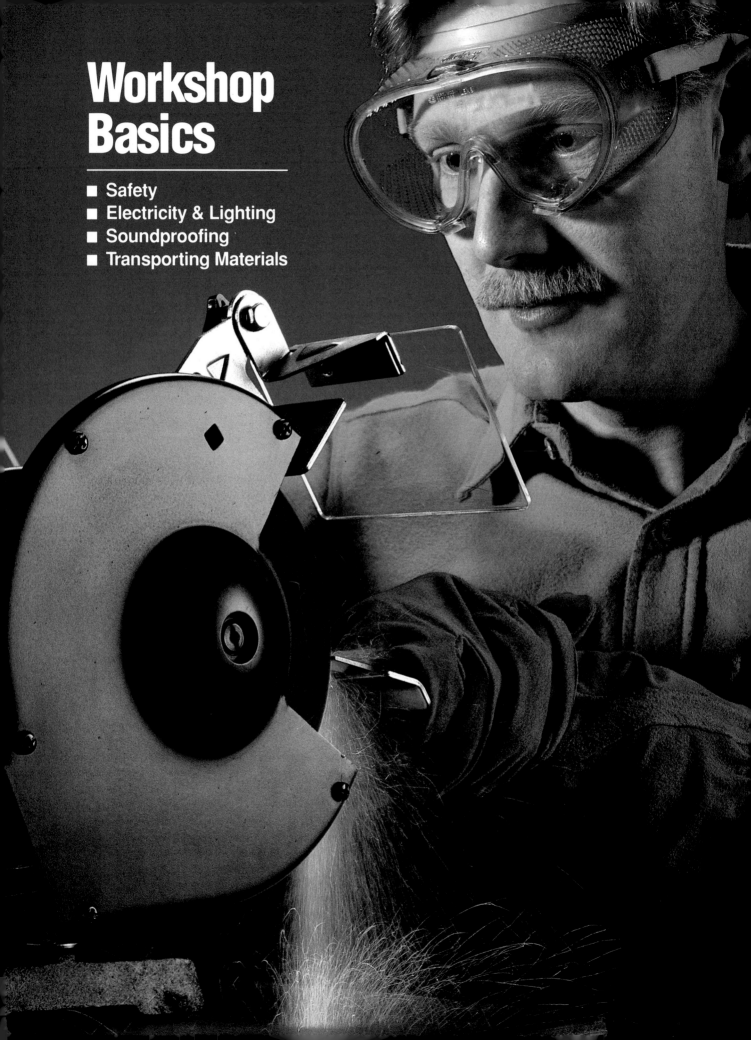

Workshop
Basics

■ Safety
■ Electricity & Lighting
■ Soundproofing
■ Transporting Materials

A functional workshop can be as small as a closet or as large as a double-car garage. It can be stocked with a few quality hand tools, or it may contain several stationary power tools costing thousands of dollars. But no matter how varied in appearance, good workshops always reflect careful thought and planning. The tips on the following pages will help you get the most out of your workshop.

When planning a new or remodeled workshop, stock it with common safety equipment. Make sure your workshop has adequate electrical service, with plenty of lighting. Consider how workshop activity affects others in the home. Make sure your shop is well ventilated, and consider soundproofing it for the comfort of others. Finally, learn how to transport building materials efficiently and safely.

Getting a Head

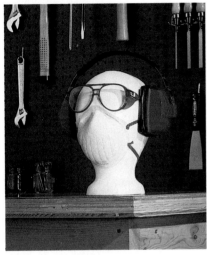

Use a rigid foam head (often used to hold wigs or hats) to store safety equipment. Put the head in a conspicuous place as a reminder to use eye protection, hearing protectors, and other safety gear.

Add-on Outlets

Your workshop should have an ample number of electrical receptacles so tools can be plugged in wherever they are needed. An easy way to add outlets to your workshop is to attach a receptacle strip to the wall above the workbench. One type of receptacle strip plugs into an existing receptacle (below), while others must be wired permanently into a circuit. Some receptacle strips have built-in circuit breakers or fuses to prevent overheating.

Get a Handle on It

Sheets of plywood are heavy and awkward to carry, even with two people. Avoid mishaps and make this job easier by attaching C-clamps to each end of the sheet to use as handles.

Put a Finish to Foot Fatigue

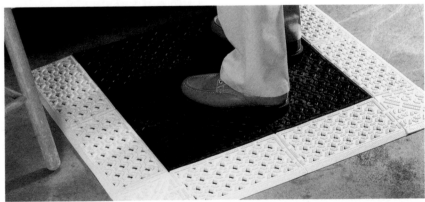

Standing on a concrete workshop floor for long periods of time can tire leg and back muscles. Fatigue also contributes to shop accidents. Reduce muscle strain by laying a resilient rubber anti-fatigue mat, available at industrial tool supply stores, on the floor in front of your work area. Or, use a scrap of old foam-backed carpeting. Wear sturdy, quality work or athletic shoes, and equip your shop with a stool to further reduce fatigue.

Take a Breather

Filter cartridges

A dual-cartridge respirator protects against toxic vapors, like those from oil-based paints and solvents, and against toxic particles, like asbestos, or sawdust from treated lumber. Correct use of the respirator can prevent lung irritations and disease. Make sure to choose a respirator that is approved by OSHA (Occupational Safety and Health Administration). Use the proper filters in the respirator cartridges, and replace them according to the manufacturer's directions.

First-aid Kit for the Shop

Keep a well-stocked basic first-aid kit where it can be reached easily. Equip your kit with a variety of bandages, needles and tweezers, antiseptic ointment, cotton swabs, cotton balls, eye drops, a first-aid handbook, a chemical cold pack, elastic bandage, first-aid tape, and sterile gauze. Seek medical help for puncture wounds, cuts, and other serious injuries.

Prevent Workshop Fires

Store flammable materials like solvents and paints in a locked metal cabinet away from sources of heat and flame. Place loose sawdust and wood chips in a covered metal trash can, and empty it frequently. Keep a fire extinguisher in the shop, and maintain it as directed by the manufacturer. Equip the workshop with a smoke detector.

Keep the Lights On

Flying wood chips from a router or power saw can shatter exposed light bulbs and fluorescent tubes. Protect light fixtures by covering them with metal window screening or wire mesh.

A Breath of Fresh Air

Ventilate your workshop so that harmful vapors and fine dust particles are blown out. Many homeowners install permanent exhaust fans, but a simple household fan placed in a window can do the job just as well. For good ventilation, your home workshop should have at least two windows, or one window and a built-in exhaust fan.

Safety Is More Than Skin Deep

Wear rubber gloves when working with solvent-based liquids. Many liquids used in the workshop are powerful skin irritants that can cause burns or blisters. Some of these materials are absorbed through the skin and have been linked to serious health problems. Disposable rubber gloves are available at pharmacies and painting supply stores. Never use gasoline or mineral spirits to clean your skin — try ordinary salad oil instead (page 120).

Stay on Your Guard

Never remove the blade guard from a table saw, radial arm saw, or other power tool. A recent survey of professional shop workers revealed that serious accidents rarely occur when blade guards are used correctly.

Key to Safe Tool Use

Prevent children from using power tools by inserting spring-metal key rings through the small holes on the prongs of the plug. Or, use small, key-operated luggage padlocks to safeguard against unauthorized tool use.

9

Make your shop safer and more convenient by using these lighting and electrical tips. Most of these improvements are easy to make, but if you are uncertain about your own skill level, have a licensed electrician make the changes.

The most common workshop electrical problem is a lack of grounded receptacles. Two-slot receptacles provide no means of grounding, and should be replaced with properly grounded three-slot receptacles. In a basement or garage, the National Electrical Code requires GFCI (ground-fault circuit-interrupter) receptacles. Install additional receptacles or add an electrical circuit if the shop is inadequately wired. A workshop should have at least one duplex receptacle for every 10 ft. of wall space.

In the Spotlight

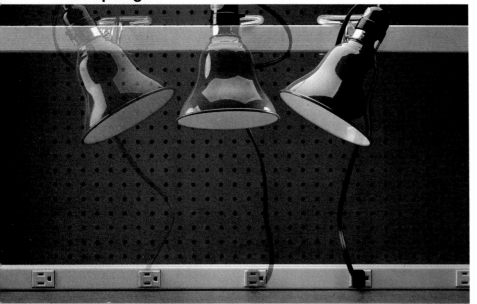

To make your shop lighting scheme more flexible, attach a 2 × 2 furring strip to the wall above the workbench, and mount a clamping arm lamp to the strip. When used with a receptacle strip (page 7), the lamp can be moved along the workbench to spotlight any work area.

Choose the Right Extension Cord (cords under 50 ft.)

Wire gauge	Watt rating	Amp rating	Typical Use
#18	600	5	Power drill, jig saw, hand sander
#16	840	7	Reciprocating saw, belt sander
#14	1440	12	Router, circular saw, miter saw, table saw
#12	1920	16	Radial arm saw, large table saw

Use only heavy-duty extension cords with large power tools. Extension cords are rated by wire gauge, watts, and amps. The smaller the wire gauge, the higher the amp and watt ratings. Make sure that the ratings of the extension cord are equal to or greater than the tool ratings. For extension cords longer than 50 ft., choose the next larger wire gauge.

Pull-apart Prevention

Prevent tool cords from pulling free of electrical extension cords by tying them in a simple knot. Knotting the cords is especially helpful when you are working on a ladder.

Prevent Electrical Shocks

Plug-in GFCI

GFCI extension cord

Although three-slot grounded receptacles provide some protection against shock, for maximum safety it is a good idea to use a GFCI (ground-fault circuit-interrupter) device in conjunction with a grounded receptacle. GFCIs sense small changes in current flow, like those that occur during a short circuit, and shut off power before a shock can occur. Common GFCI devices include plug-in portable GFCIs and GFCI extension cords. To make your own GFCI extension cord, see pages 12 to 13.

Brighter Lights, Smaller Electrical Bills

Improve visibility in your shop by replacing incandescent lights with fluorescent fixtures. Fluorescent lights provide more light than incandescent lights and are less expensive to operate. Some types of fluorescent light fixtures come with preattached cords for plugging into a receptacle. Other types are permanently wired; you may want to hire an electrician to make permanent installations.

More Power to You

If you are upgrading your electrical service, have an electrician install a subpanel near the shop to control the circuits that serve it. A nearby subpanel is convenient if a circuit breaker trips or a fuse blows. With a subpanel, you can also turn off workshop circuits and lock the subpanel cover to prevent unauthorized tool use.

Dust Caps for Receptacles

Cover unused receptacles by inserting plastic caps into the slots. The caps will keep sawdust and dirt from clogging the receptacle slots—a common cause of short circuits and workshop fires.

Reel Convenience

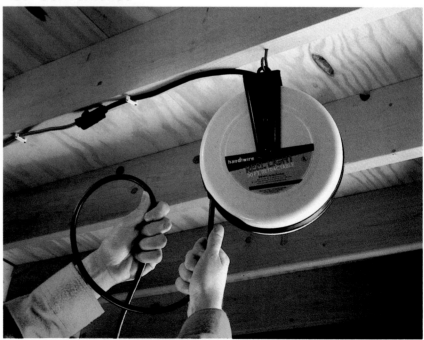

Prevent extension cord tangles by hanging retractable or reel-type extension cords from overhead hooks. They can be positioned wherever they are needed, and retracted when not in use. Retractable cords are available in lengths ranging from 10 to 30 ft.

A GFCI extension cord provides extra protection against shock, making it a good choice when working outdoors or in damp locations, where shocks are more likely to occur.

Make a GFCI Extension Cord for Low-cost Shock Protection

If a permanently wired GFCI receptacle is not available, use a GFCI extension cord whenever working outdoors or in damp locations. A GFCI extension cord has a built-in ground-fault circuit-interrupter to reduce the chance of shock.

GFCI extension cords can be purchased, but it is cheaper to make your own. Adding a switch to the extension cord lets you shut off power on-site without unplugging the cord. You can also use the cord as an accessory for a portable workbench (page 32).

Everything You Need:

Tools: linesman's pliers, utility knife, screwdriver, combination tool.

Materials: 12-gauge grounded extension cord, cable clamp, 4" × 4" metal electrical box (2⅛" deep) with extension ring and grounding screw, GFCI receptacle, single-pole wall switch with grounding screw, 6" length of 12-gauge black wire, three grounding pigtails, wire nut, plastic coverplate.

How to Make a GFCI Extension Cord

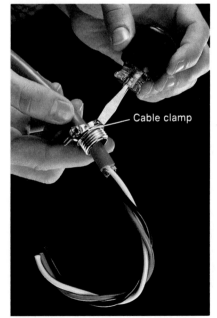

Cable clamp

1 Cut off slotted receptacle end of the extension cord with a linesman's pliers. Strip 8" of outer insulation from the cord, using a utility knife. Thread the cord through a cable clamp, and tighten the clamp with a screwdriver.

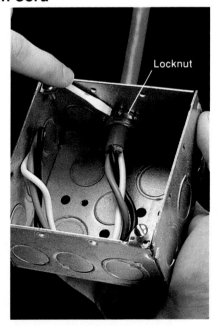

Locknut

2 Insert the cable clamp into one of the knockouts on the electrical box. Screw a locknut onto the cable clamp, and tighten it by pushing against the locknut lugs with a screwdriver.

3 Strip about ¾" of plastic insulation from each wire in the box, using a combination tool.

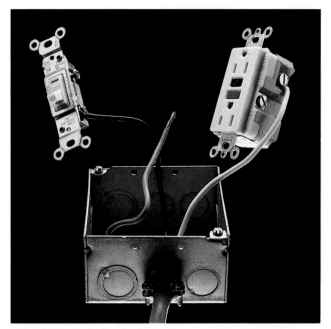

4 Connect the white wire to the silver screw terminal marked LINE on the GFCI, wrapping the stripped portion of the wire around the screw in a clockwise direction. Tighten the screw terminal with a screwdriver. Attach the black wire to one of the brass screw terminals on the single-pole switch.

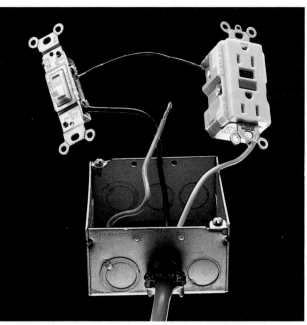

5 Strip ¾" of insulation from both ends of a 6" length of 12-gauge black wire. Connect one end of the wire to the remaining brass screw terminal on the switch, and connect the other end to the brass screw terminal marked LINE on the GFCI.

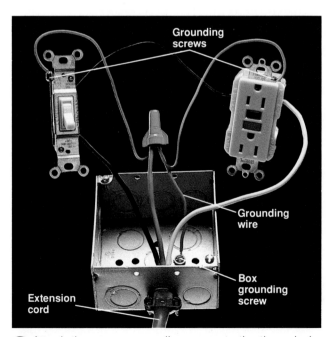

Grounding screws

Grounding wire

Box grounding screw

Extension cord

6 Attach the green grounding screw to the threaded hole in the back of the box, and attach a grounding pigtail to the screw. Attach additional grounding pigtails to the grounding screws on the switch and the receptacle. Join the pigtails and the extension cord grounding wire with a green wire nut.

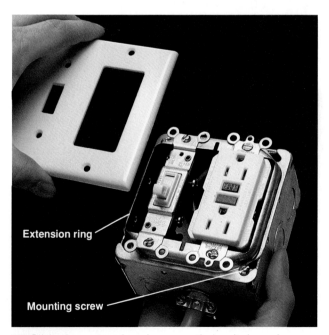

Extension ring

Mounting screw

7 Slide the extension ring over the switch and receptacle, and attach it to the box with mounting screws. Carefully tuck the wires into the box, and secure the switch and receptacle to the extension ring. Attach the plastic coverplate.

The noise generated by some power tools, like circular saws or routers, can reach 115 decibels, enough to cause pain and permanent hearing loss to the listener. Reduce noise hazards by wearing hearing protectors whenever using power tools. Remember, however, that workshop noise is heard easily in other parts of the home. For the comfort and safety of family members, soundproof your shop to muffle the noise.

Noise levels in a home workshop can be controlled by reducing the sound-causing vibrations of power tools. Or, you can soundproof walls and ceilings to prevent noise from being carried to other parts of the home.

Wall constructions are rated for noise by the Sound Transmission Class (STC) system. The higher the STC rating of a wall, the less sound it will transmit. The chart (page opposite) shows different wall constructions, and rates their ability to carry sound.

Deaden Your Doors

Workshop doors with hollow-core construction carry sound well. Deaden sound transmission through a door by attaching acoustical tile to the inside surface. The tiled door surface also can be used as a bulletin board.

Seal Sound Gaps

Air gaps in walls and ceilings can carry sound. To limit the amount of noise (and dust) escaping to other rooms, install door sweeps to seal the gaps underneath workshop doors, install insulating gaskets around electrical outlets, and use fiberglass insulation to plug the holes near water pipes and the spaces between ceiling joists.

Stop Bad Vibes

Motor vibrations carried through metal tool legs to a work surface or floor can increase workshop noise levels. When clamping a tool to a workbench, stop noisy vibrations by placing pads of rubber, pieces of carpet, or rubber furniture cups between the tool legs and bench. Power tool legs that rest directly on the floor also can be padded to reduce vibrations. Also keep tools well oiled to further reduce noise.

Soundproofing Walls & Ceilings (walls shown cut away)	Sound Transmission Class & Comfort Level in Adjacent Room
Typical utility-area stud wall, unfinished on one side.	**STC 28** Power tool noise is loud enough to cause permanent hearing loss with prolonged exposure.
Finish the workshop side of wall with ½" wallboard (A).	**STC 34**
Fill spaces between framing members with fiberglass insulation (B) and cover stud wall with wallboard.	**STC 39**
Add an extra layer of wallboard (C) to the workshop side of the insulated stud wall.	**STC 42**
Attach an extra layer of wallboard to wall, using resilient steel channels (D). Attach channels every 24".	**STC 44**
Attach acoustical tile (E) to the insulated stud wall, using construction adhesive or staples.	**STC 46**
Attach ½" Sound Stop® board (F) and an extra layer of wallboard to walls.	**STC 50** Power tool noise is barely audible.

15

Transporting building materials from the lumberyard or home center to your home is the first step in any workshop project— and it may be the most difficult. Framing lumber can be tied to a roof carrier rack for transporting, but sheets of plywood, paneling, or wallboard should be delivered by truck. Your lumberyard may deliver your materials for a small additional charge.

If you transport materials on a roof carrier, make sure to tie the load securely (page opposite). Materials that extend past the rear bumper should be tagged with a red flag to warn drivers behind you. Drive carefully and avoid sudden starts and stops. When using your vehicle to carry heavy loads, like bags of concrete or sand, allow extra braking distance.

All by Yourself

To carry full-size sheets of plywood, paneling, or wallboard by yourself, tie a single length of rope, about 18 ft. long, in a loop. Hook the ends of the loop over the lower corners of the sheet, and grip the middle of the rope in one hand. Use the other hand to balance the sheet.

Cut Problems Down to Size

If you already know the cutting dimensions for plywood, paneling, or other sheet goods, you can make transportation easier by cutting the materials to size while still at the lumberyard or home center. Some lumberyards will cut your materials free of charge. Or, you can bring along a saw and cut the materials yourself.

Up on the Roof

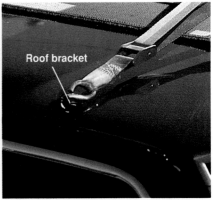

Roof bracket

Tie materials onto the roof of your car using inexpensive, vinyl-coated roof brackets. Hook the brackets over the edge of the roof, then attach nylon packing straps or ropes to the brackets for cinching materials in place. Place carpet scraps under the materials to prevent scratches, and center the load on the car roof.

How to Tie a Load onto an Auto Roof Carrier

1 Tie a half hitch around one end of the roof carrier bar. Pull the knot tight.

2 Tie a second half hitch in the rope, and pull the knot tight. A half hitch has good holding power, yet is easy to untie.

3 Pull the rope over the top of the load. If possible, wrap the rope once around the load. Tie a small slip loop in the rope.

4 Stretch the rope around the opposite end of the roof carrier bar.

5 Thread the end of the rope through the slip loop. Pull the rope firmly against the loop to cinch the load tight against the roof carrier.

6 Tie off the rope below the slip loop, using half hitches. Repeat steps 1 to 6 at the other carrier bar. If desired, large loads also can be tied to the front and rear bumpers of the car, using the same rope technique.

Workshop Organization

- Storage
- Carousel Shelf
- Fold-down Workshelf
- Mini Workbench
- Router Worktop

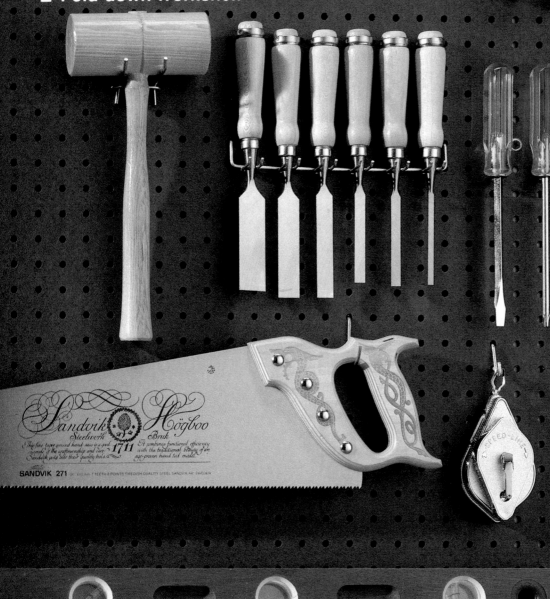

Most home workshops must fit into an unused utility space—often a cramped area tucked into a basement, garage, or attic. Creating work space and storage areas for tools and materials is a constant challenge. The following pages show you dozens of easy ways to solve common storage problems and organize a new or existing workshop for maximum efficiency. By investing one or two weekends of your time and using inexpensive materials like pegboard, you can turn any cluttered utility area into a functional, enjoyable home workshop.

Pegboard Storage Panel for Stud Walls

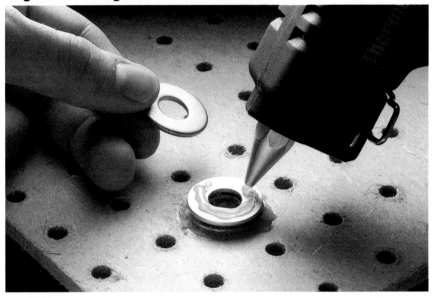

When attaching a pegboard panel to finished walls, hot-glue pairs of washers to the back of the pegboard as spacers, so that pegboard hooks can be inserted. Hang the pegboard panel by anchoring it to every other wall stud, using 2" wallboard screws. Use finish washers (step 3, below) to keep the screw heads from sinking into the pegboard.

Tool Templates

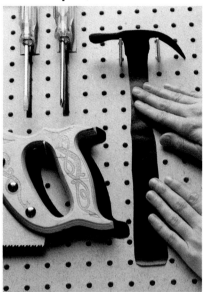

Tool outlines made from contact paper or cardboard can be attached to a pegboard storage panel so tools can be returned to the correct locations after use.

Pegboard Storage Panel for Masonry Walls

Finish washer

1 When attaching pegboard to masonry walls, first measure and cut 1" × 2" furring strips to match the height of the pegboard panel. Apply panel adhesive to one side of each strip. Adhesive will help hold furring strips to the masonry walls.

2 Attach furring strips to wall with 2" masonry nails. For solid support, space the strips no more than 4 ft. apart. For example, a 6-ft.-long pegboard panel requires one furring strip for each end, plus a third strip to support the middle of the panel.

3 Position the pegboard panel against the furring strips. Drive ¾" wallboard screws through the pegboard holes and into the furring strips. Use finish washers to keep the heads of the wallboard screws from sinking into the pegboard.

Use Plastic Bottles for Workshop Storage

Keep clean rags handy for painting and finishing projects by storing them in plastic containers hung from a pegboard storage panel. Rags soaked in mineral spirits or other solvent-based liquids pose a fire hazard. Let dirty rags dry outdoors, then throw them away with household trash.

Storing Saw Accessories

Attach pegboard to the sides of a table saw stand to create storage space for spare saw blades, adjustment wrenches, and other table saw accessories. Attach the pegboard by drilling holes in the legs of the saw stand and mounting the pegboard panel with machine screws and nuts.

Make a Saw Blade Caddy

Use a plywood scrap to make a convenient caddy for storing saw blades and carrying them to a job site. Use a jig saw to cut a carrying handle in the top of the plywood. Drill a 3/8" hole through the center of the plywood, and secure the blades with a 3" carriage bolt, wing nut, and washer. Place cardboard between the blades to protect the teeth from damage.

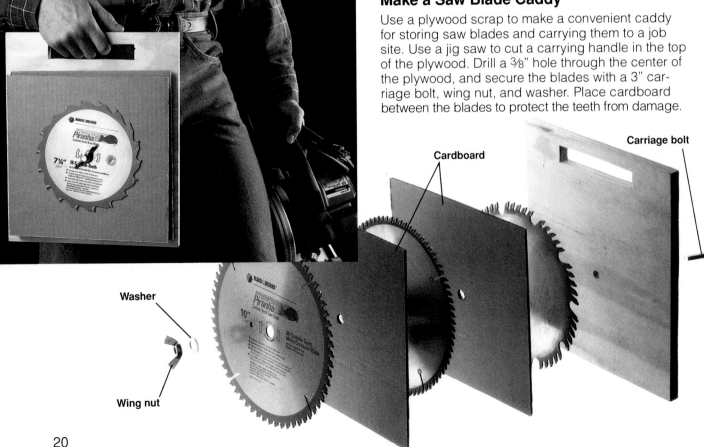

Cardboard

Carriage bolt

Washer

Wing nut

Bench Buddy

Create more storage space by at-taching pieces of pegboard to the sides of the workbench with wall-board screws and finish washers.

Hide-away Hangers

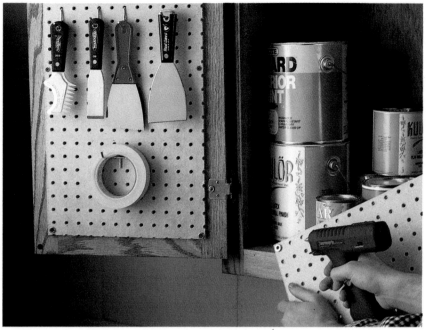

The inside surface of cabinet doors is an overlooked storage area. To make use of this space, attach small pegboard panels with ½" wallboard screws. Glue pairs of metal washers on the back of the pegboard as spacers to provide room for pegboard hooks to be inserted (page 19).

Bit by Bit

Metal drill and router bits have finely honed cutting edges which can be ruined if the bits bump against each other inside a toolbox or work-bench drawer. To protect tool bits from damage, make a storage block by boring holes in a scrap piece of lumber. Attach screw eyes to the top of the block so it can be stored on pegboard hooks and taken down when a bit is needed.

Up Against the Wall

Add storage space in an un-finished utility area by covering the studs with panels of peg-board. These panels are ideal for storing wallboard framing squares, levels, garden tools, and other large items.

Stick 'em Up

Attach magnetic strips to the front of a workbench to store small metal tools, hardware items, tool wrenches, or drill chuck keys. Magnetic strips also can be attached to a metal table saw stand or other stationary tool. You can purchase these powerful magnetic strips at hardware or cutlery stores.

Keep Your Cap On

The caps that come with glues, caulks, and other shop products are easy to lose. Replace lost caps with screw-on electrical wire nuts. Wire nuts, available in many sizes, can be purchased at any hardware store.

Glued Clues

Most workshops have dozens of small containers holding screws, nails, bolts, and other hardware. To locate items quickly and easily, use a hot glue gun to stick a sample of the contents on the outside of each bag or box.

Sanding Belt Storage

Sanding belts stored in a drawer or toolbox can get creased or flattened and lose their effectiveness. To avoid this, hang sanding belts from old paint-roller covers or pieces of PVC plumbing pipe attached to pegboard hooks.

Fallout Protection

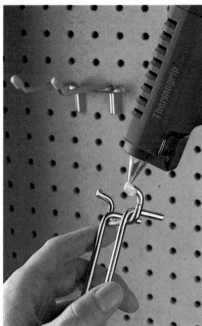

Pegboard hooks frequently fall out when an item is removed. End this aggravating problem by gluing the hooks to the pegboard with a hot glue gun. If you need to reposition the pegboard hooks, heat them for a few seconds with a heat gun until the glue softens.

Beat the Tangle Tussle

Extension cords and power tool cords often become knotted and tangled. To keep a cord neatly coiled, cut off the ends of a clean plastic motor oil bottle, and slip it over the coiled electrical cord. Or secure cords with the ties from plastic garbage bags.

Out of Sight, Easy to Find

Make use of storage space underneath a stairway. Build a simple plywood shelf and attach it to the stairway stringers to store tool manuals, small cans, and bottles. Attach nails and hooks to risers for storing rolls of tape, paint brushes, putty knives, and other small tools.

Rack 'em Up

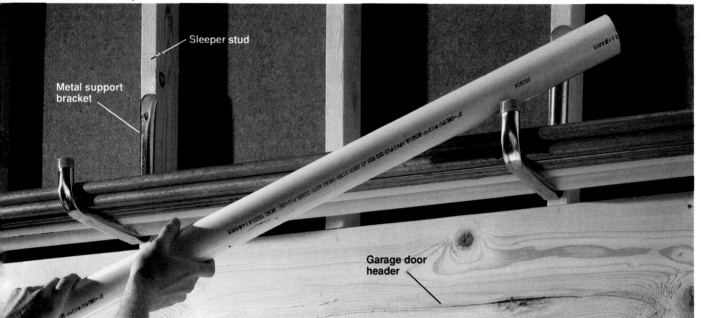

Sleeper stud

Metal support
bracket

Garage door
header

The inside wall above a garage door makes a good storage space. Use this area to store long pieces of wood molding, dimension lumber, or plumbing pipe. Attach metal or wooden support brackets to the sleeper studs or header. Metal brackets, available at any hardware store or home center, can be attached to the front of sleeper studs with long wallboard screws or lag screws. Or, cut L-shaped wooden brackets from scrap plywood, and attach them to the sides of the sleeper studs with 2" wallboard screws. To provide adequate support, space the brackets no more than 36" apart.

Up, Up & Away

Furring
strip

Store long materials in the space between open ceiling joists in an unfinished utility area like a garage or basement. Attach ¾" plywood furring strips across the joists with 2½" wallboard screws or lag screws. Space the strips no more than 36" apart to provide adequate support. Make sure to avoid any electrical cables or fixtures located between the ceiling joists. Some homeowners attach boards across the bottom of the ceiling joists to make out-of-the-way storage shelves for small cans and other shop items.

Waste-not Storage Boxes

Use leftover pieces of plywood or 1" lumber to build sturdy storage boxes for heavy hardware. Assemble the boxes with 1¼" wallboard screws. Organize the storage boxes on utility shelves for easy access. If you wish, attach metal handles to the boxes. Wooden drawers from a discarded desk or dresser also make good storage boxes.

Hang 'em High

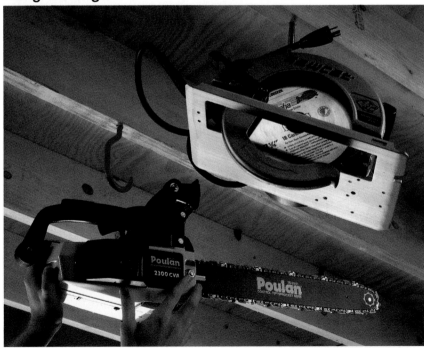

Use large, rubber-coated lag hooks to store power tools off the floor and away from dirt and moisture. Anchor the lag hooks securely to ceiling joists or cross blocking.

How to Coil Long Extension Cords

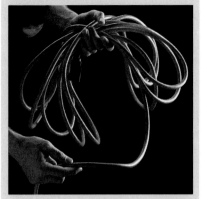

1 Hold the end of the extension cord in one hand. Use the other hand to loop the extension cord back and forth in a figure-eight pattern until it is completely coiled.

2 Take one of the cord loops and wrap it twice around one end of the coil.

3 Insert the loop though the center of the coil, and pull it tight. Store the cord by hanging it from this loop.

Clever Cord Carrier

Keep extension cords tangle-free by storing them in 5-gallon plastic buckets. Cut a hole in the side of the bucket near the bottom. Thread the pronged extension cord plug through the hole from the inside, then coil the cord into the bucket. The extension cord will remain tangle-free when pulled from the bucket. You can also use the bucket to carry tools to a work site.

Bit Bed

Protect and organize expensive router bits by lining a workbench drawer with rigid foam or foam rubber. Cut out recesses in the foam so the finely honed cutting edges do not bump against other objects.

Pipe Dream

Organize a collection of pipe clamps and bar clamps by storing them on a 2 × 4 attached to wall studs. Anchor the 2 × 4 to the studs with 3" wallboard screws or lag screws.

Make Use of Wasted Space by Building a Carousel Shelf

A carousel shelf improves access to cramped areas, like the space underneath a stairway. The turntable bearing used for this project is available at woodworking stores.

Everything You Need:

Tools: pencil, drill, bits (⅜" masonry, ¾" spade), hammer, screwdriver.

Materials: 12" turntable bearing, plastic masonry anchors, ¾" plywood disk (3-ft. diameter), ¾" wallboard screws, #8 × 1½" sheet-metal screws.

How to Install a Carousel Shelf on a Concrete Floor

1 Position the turntable bearing on the floor. Locate the holes for masonry anchors by rotating the bearing and marking the floor through the large access opening in the top of the bearing.

2 Remove the turntable bearing and drill 2"-deep anchor holes at the marked points, using a ⅜" masonry bit. Insert the masonry anchors into the floor holes.

3 Position the bearing upside down on the plywood disk, making sure it is centered. Mark location of large access opening on disk. Remove the bearing, and drill a ¾" access hole in disk. Reposition bearing and attach it to disk with ¾" wallboard screws.

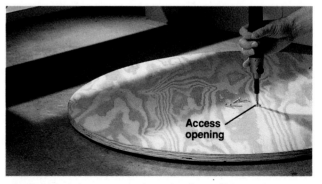

4 Position the carousel on the floor. Rotate the plywood disk, and drive 1½" sheet-metal screws into the floor anchors through the access opening.

Save Space by Building a Fold-down Workshelf

Make the most of limited workshop space by building a fold-down worksshelf. The worksshelf can be mounted from exposed wall studs, or from a frame attached to masonry walls. When it is not in use, fold the worksshelf up and out of the way.

This plan is for a 24" × 30" worksshelf attached to masonry walls, but the design can be changed to meet your workshop needs. For clearance, the shelf width should be ½" less than the space between the framing members. If desired, install pegboard storage panels between the framing members.

Everything You Need:

Tools: tape measure, pencil, saw, drill, drill bits (⅜" spade, ⅝" masonry, ⅛" twist), level, hammer, caulk gun, ratchet wrench, screwdriver.

Materials: three 6-ft. 2 × 4s, one 8-ft. 2 × 4, four ⅝" masonry anchors, panel adhesive, four ⅜" × 6" lag screws with washers, ¾" plywood (24" × 30"), four ⅜" × 5" carriage bolts with washers and nuts, 2" wallboard screws, two 3" hinges, two ⅜" × 4" bolts with washers and nuts, ⅜" dowel (3" long).

Lumber Cutting List

Key	Number of Pieces	Size and Description of Pieces
A	2	2 × 4 workshelf framing members, 6 ft. long
B	2	2 × 4 workshelf sides, 24" long, cut as shown
C	1	¾" plywood shelf, 24" × 30"
D	1	2 × 4 shelf support, 30" long
E	2	2 × 4 legs, 32" long

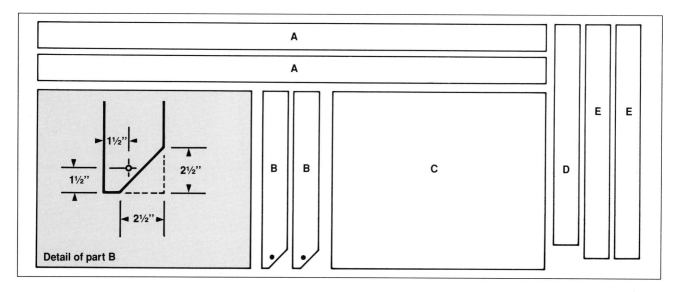

Detail of part B

How to Build a Fold-down Workshelf

1 Set the framing members (A) on edge, and drill two holes down through each piece, using a ⅜" spade bit. Position one of the holes 18" from the end of the 2 × 4, and position the other hole 36" from the first hole.

2 Position framing members against the wall, and mark hole locations for the masonry anchors, using a pencil. Framing members should be spaced 32" apart (on-center), and must be plumb. Drill 2"-deep holes in the wall, using a ⅝" masonry bit.

3 Tap a ⅝" masonry anchor into each hole. Apply a thick bead of panel adhesive to the back of each framing member. Anchor the framing members to the walls with ⅜" × 6" lag screws and washers, using a ratchet wrench.

(continued next page)

How to Build a Fold-down Worksheet (continued)

4 Position the worksheet sides (B) on edge, and drill two ⅜" holes down through each piece. Position one hole 4½" from the angled end of the 2 × 4, and position the other hole 2½" from the square end.

5 Lay the worksheet sides flat. On each piece, mark a point 1½" from the angled end of the 2 × 4 and 1½" from the bottom edge (see detail of part B, page 29). Drill a ⅜" hole at each point.

6 Position the worksheet sides on the plywood shelf (C), with the edges flush and the square ends facing the same direction. Use a pencil to mark hole locations on plywood. Remove the sides, and drill ⅜" holes through plywood.

7 Insert ⅜" × 5" carriage bolts through the work-shelf sides and the plywood shelf. Join the pieces together with washers and nuts, and tighten with a ratchet wrench.

8 Set the worksheet upside down. Position the shelf support (D) on the bottom of the worksheet, about 5" from the front edge. Attach the shelf support with 2" wallboard screws driven every 8".

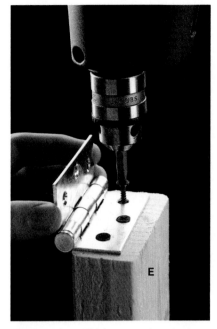

9 Attach a 3" hinge to the end of each leg (E), using 2" wallboard screws. The edge of the leg should be flush with the edge of the hinge pin. Drill 1/8" pilot holes to prevent screws from splitting the wood at the end grain.

10 Attach the legs to the workshelf by screwing the hinges to the shelf support with 2" wallboard screws. The hinge pins should just touch the back edge of the shelf support.

11 Drill a 3/8" mounting hole in the center of each framing member, 36" above the floor.

12 Position the workshelf between the framing members, and attach it with 3/8" × 4" bolts, washers, and nuts. Tighten the nuts with a ratchet wrench until snug.

13 Raise the workshelf to the upright (closed) position. Make a shelf lock by drilling a 3/8" hole through one of the framing members and partway into the side of the shelf. Insert a 3" length of 3/8" dowel to keep the workshelf in the upright position when not in use.

The basic mini workbench design has flush edges that allow clamping from many positions. The cutout top lets you support workpieces so drill bits and saw blades will not damage the bench (photo, left).

The solid worktop attaches to the workbench with machine screws and wing nuts. It provides a smooth work surface for assembling, painting, and gluing.

A router worktop attaches to the cutout bench top, turning your mini workbench into a router table.

Save Space by Building a Mini Workbench with Interchangeable Worktops

This mini workbench requires only 3 sq. ft. of floor space, and is easy to store and move. It is ideal for cramped work spaces. Taller than most portable workbenches, the mini workbench raises projects to a comfortable working height. It includes two shelves for storing tools, materials, and accessories.

The mini workbench features a cutout top that supports your work so a drill or jig saw will not damage the bench top. To make the workbench more versatile, you can build interchangeable tops, like the solid worktop (page 35) and router worktop (pages 36 to 37).

Everything You Need:

Tools: saw, tape measure, combination square, pencil, drill, drill bits (5/32", 3/16" twist, 3/4" spade, countersink), power screwdriver, jig saw, clamp.

Materials: three 2 × 4s (8 ft. long), 1/2 sheet of 3/4" or 1/2" plywood, 1/2" finish plywood (22" × 26"), wallboard screws (2 1/2", 1 1/4"), four 3/16" × 2" flat-head machine screws with washers and wing nuts.

Lumber Cutting List

Key	Pcs	Description
A	4	2 x 4 legs, 40" long
B	4	2 x 4 rails, 18" long
C	2	2 x 4 shelf supports, 19" long
D	1	Plywood back, 22" × 24"
E	2	Plywood shelves, 18" × 19"
F	1	Plywood bench top, 18" × 22"
G	1	½" finish-plywood worktop, 22" × 26"

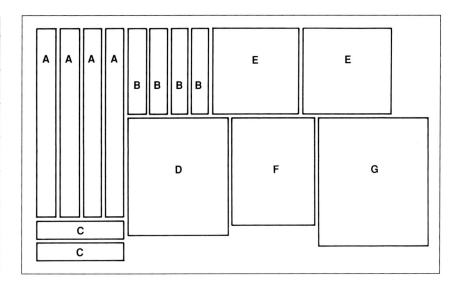

How to Build a Mini Workbench

1 Mark one end of each of the four legs (A) as the "bottom." Measure up from the bottoms of the legs and mark points at 1½" and 5". At these marks, use a combination square to draw lines across the legs to serve as reference marks for attaching the bottom rails.

2 Drill two 5⁄32" pilot holes at both ends of each rail (B). Offset the holes slightly for maximum holding power, and make sure they are no more than 3" from the end of the board.

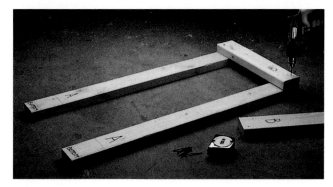

3 Lay two legs flat, and place a rail (B) across the top of the legs, flush with the edges. Join the pieces by driving a single 2½" wallboard screw through the rail and into each leg. Position another rail across the bottom of the legs, between the reference lines, and attach with 2½" wallboard screws.

4 Check for squareness by measuring the diagonals, W-X and Y-Z. If necessary, twist the frame until diagonal measurements are identical. Drive screws into the remaining pilot holes. Repeat steps 3 and 4 for the remaining set of rails and legs.

(continued next page)

How to Build a Mini Workbench (continued)

5 Lay the leg assemblies flat, with the rails facing down. Measuring from the bottom, make reference marks at 25½" and 29" on the outside edge of each leg. At the marked points, draw perpendicular reference lines across the legs. These lines will be used when attaching shelf supports.

6 Drill two ⁵⁄₃₂" pilot holes between each pair of reference lines. Position the holes ¾" from the outside edges of the legs, so that the holes will be centered on the shelf supports.

7 Set leg assemblies on edge with rails facing each other. Position the shelf supports (C) between leg assemblies so ends are between reference lines. Make sure the shelf supports are flush with outside edges of the legs. Attach the shelf supports to the legs with 2½" wallboard screws.

8 Place the workbench back (D) on the workbench frame so it is flush with the edge of the shelf support. Check the frame for squareness (step 4, page 33), then attach the back to the workbench frame with 1¼" wallboard screws driven every 6".

9 Stand the workbench upright. Position one shelf (E) on the bottom rails and the other shelf on the shelf supports. Attach the shelves to the supports and rails with 1¼" wallboard screws driven every 6".

10 Lay the bench top (F) flat, and draw a line on each short side, 2¼" from the edge. Drill three evenly spaced ⁵⁄₃₂" pilot holes on each line, then countersink each hole.

11 Position the bench top on the workbench frame, and make sure the edges are flush with the outside corners of the legs. Attach the bench top by driving 1¼" wallboard screws through the pilot holes and into the frame.

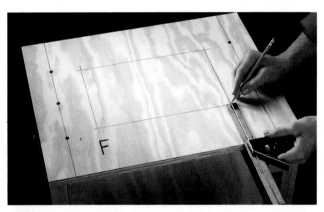

12 Set the combination square blade to a depth of 5". Draw a line parallel to each edge of the bench top, using the combination square as a guide.

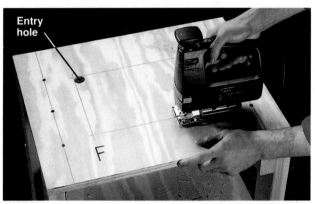

13 Cut out the center rectangle formed by the lines, using a jig saw. Start the cut by drilling ¾" entry holes at opposite corners.

Make the solid worktop (G) by centering it on the bench so it overhangs by 2" on all sides. Clamp it in place, then mark four corner points, each located 6" in from the edges. Drill a ³⁄₁₆" mounting hole through the worktop and the bench top at each corner mark. Countersink all holes.

Mount the solid worktop by inserting a ³⁄₁₆" × 2" flat-head machine screw into each mounting hole and securing the worktop with washers and wing nuts. The worktop can be removed for quick and easy access to the cutout bench top.

Turn Your Mini Workbench into a Router Table

You can turn your mini workbench into a router table with this easy-to-make router worktop. A router table is convenient for repetitive work or for routing small workpieces. The router worktop design includes an adjustable fence to help guide workpieces across the router bit.

To make safe, accurate cuts with the mini workbench router table, use fingerboards (pages 64 to 65). Fingerboards keep a workpiece snug against the worktop fence during cutting.

Everything You Need:

Tools: clamps, drill, drill bits ($\frac{3}{16}$", $\frac{5}{32}$", $\frac{3}{8}$" twist, countersink), pencil, compass, jig saw with scrolling blade, power screwdriver.

Materials: $\frac{1}{2}$" finish plywood (24" × 28"); $\frac{3}{4}$" plywood (8" × 28"); $\frac{3}{16}$" flat-head machine screws with washers, wing nuts; $1\frac{1}{4}$" wallboard screws.

Lumber Cutting List

Key	Pcs	Description
A	1	$\frac{1}{2}$" finish-plywood top (24" × 28")
B	1	$\frac{3}{4}$" plywood fence guide (4" × 28")
C	1	$\frac{3}{4}$" plywood fence bottom (4" × 28")

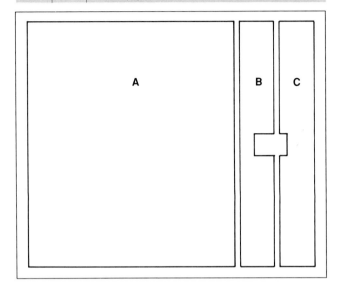

How to Build a Router Worktop

1 Center top (A) on bench and clamp in position. From underneath, locate mounting holes in the bench top; drill $\frac{3}{16}$" holes up through worktop. From top side, countersink the mounting holes. Attach worktop to bench, using $\frac{3}{16}$" flat-head machine screws with washers and wing nuts.

2 Draw diagonal lines across the worktop from opposite corners. At the intersection of the lines, use a compass to mark a 2"-diameter hole. Drill a $\frac{3}{8}$" pilot hole, then cut out the circle using a jig saw and a fine-tooth scrolling blade.

3 Remove the mounting screws in baseplate of router. Remove the baseplate, and position it over the 2" hole in the worktop. Mark the locations of the baseplate mounting screws on the worktop. Drill $\frac{3}{16}$" mounting holes at the marks, and countersink all holes. Store the router baseplate.

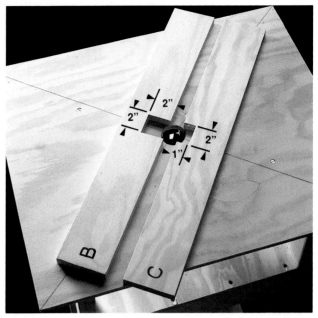

4 Position the router underneath the worktop so the holes in the router base line up with the mounting holes in the worktop. Attach the router to the worktop with the baseplate mounting screws. Make sure the screws are tight.

5 Cut a 2"-square notch in the center of the fence guide (B). Cut a notch in the center of the fence bottom (C) 1" deep and 2" wide.

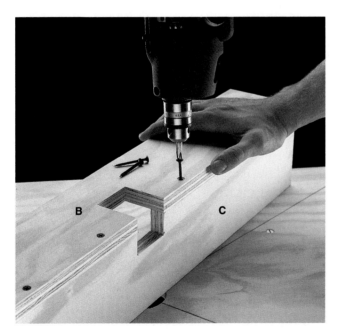

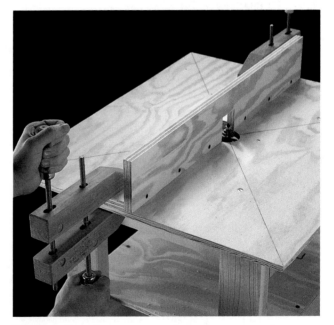

6 Turn the fence bottom (C) on edge, with the notched side up. Position the fence guide (B) on top of the fence bottom, so that the ends and edges are flush and the notches are aligned. Drill six evenly spaced 5⁄32" pilot holes through the fence guide, and countersink all holes. Join the pieces with 1¼" wallboard screws.

When using the router worktop, clamp the fence securely to the worktop so the notch is around the router bit. You may want to make a GFCI extension cord (pages 12 to 13), and mount it on the workbench. The extension cord has a convenient switch for turning the router on and off.

Tools

- Hammers
- Drills
- Handsaws
- Chisels & Planes
- Homemade Tools

- Circular Saws
- Routers
- Table Saws
- Power Miter Saws

The following pages offer nearly 100 tips to help you get the most out of your hand and power tools.

Some hand tools can be modified to make convenient specialty tools. You can also build your own tool accessories, including a variety of cutting guides, to help make routine workshop tasks quicker and easier.

Tools must be kept clean and dry, and cutting blades should be sharpened regularly. Properly maintained, good-quality tools can last a lifetime.

Take the time to learn how to use your tools correctly. Practice your tool techniques on scrap materials, and consult a tool-use book or ask an experienced friend for advice if you are unsure of your skills.

Conquer Rust

Remove rust from metal surfaces with steel wool, using light machine oil as a lubricant. As you remove rust, wipe the spot frequently with a clean cloth to remove rust particles and steel wool fragments. Coat surfaces with light oil to prevent further rusting.

Rust Buster

Store hand tools in a drawer lined with a piece of scrap carpet moistened with light machine oil. The carpet prevents tools from getting scratched or nicked, and the oil prevents rusting. Discard the carpet if it becomes caked with sawdust and dirt.

Less Wetter Is Better

Use a dehumidifier to control dampness in a basement or other shop location. High humidity levels cause rust to form on tool surfaces and inside power tool motors.

Tale of the Tape

Coat the blade of a steel tape measure with paste wax. The wax keeps the tape retractor working smoothly, and prevents dirt and grease from sticking to the blade.

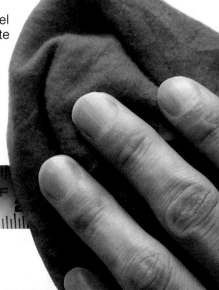

Two Claws in One

Small finish nails and brads can be difficult to pull with an ordinary hammer. Turn your claw hammer into a mini nail-puller by filing a ⅛" notch into one claw, using a triangular needle file (inset).

Grain of Truth

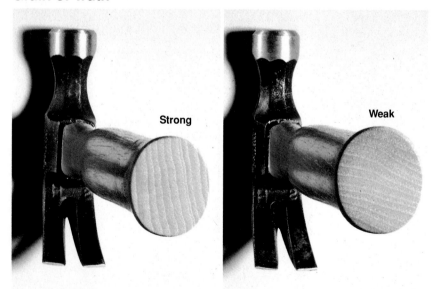

The strongest wooden tool handles have wood grain that runs parallel to the tool head (left). Handles with the grain running perpendicular to the tool head (right) are more likely to break. Check the end grain before buying a new tool or tool handle. Tool handles that are cracked or loose should be replaced.

Thumbs Up

To avoid hitting your thumb when hammering a small nail, push the nail through a piece of stiff paper, or hold it with a needlenose pliers or tweezers.

Easy Driver

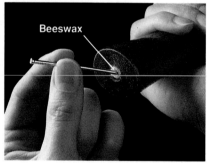

Beeswax

Drive nails into hard woods more easily by lubricating the nail points with beeswax. Keep a supply of wax handy by drilling a ¼" hole, ½" deep, in the end of your hammer handle and filling the hole with wax.

More Power to You

Remove stubborn nails by placing a block of wood under the hammer head for added leverage. Prevent damage to the workpiece by using a block big enough to distribute the pressure from the hammer head.

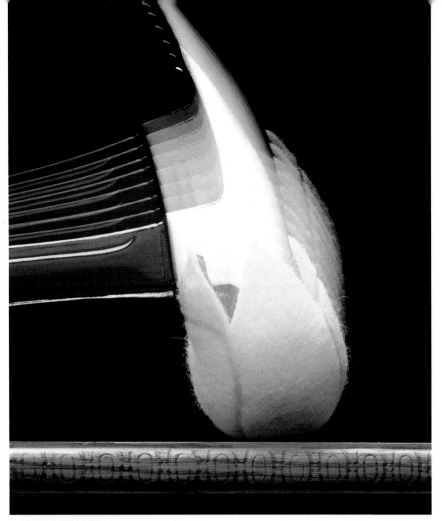

One-handed Nail Starter

Some situations require starting nails with one hand. Do this by wedging the nail in the claws so the nail head rests against the hammer head. Swing the hammer with the claws facing forward to start the nail, then loosen the claws from the nail and finish driving the nail with the striking face.

Soften the Blow

Using a standard metal hammer to tap wood joints into place can damage the workpiece. To avoid marring workpieces, convert your hammer to a soft-headed mallet. Cut a slit in a tennis ball, and slip it over the striking face of the hammer.

Surface Saver

Protect surfaces from hammer misses by slipping a piece of scrap pegboard over the nail and against the workpiece. When the nail is flush to the surface of the pegboard, remove the pegboard and finish the job with a nail set. Keep the striking face of the hammer clean by rubbing it with fine sandpaper. This will keep the face from slipping off the nail head.

Pulling Headless Nails

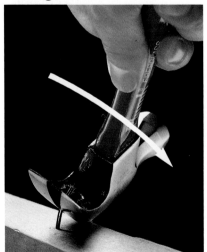

Pull headless nails by wedging the shank of the nail tightly in the claws and levering the hammer handle sideways. Inside edges of the claws must be sharp.

Sharpen Your Claws

Sharpen here

Inspect the hammer claws to make sure the tips and inside edges are sharp enough to grip nails. Sharpen dull claws with a flat metal file.

Bit Saver

Because thin twist bits can bend and break easily, use a finish nail to bore pilot holes when installing molding and doing other rough work. Cut off the nail head with a side cutter, and insert the nail into the drill chuck. Save expensive twist bits for fine work.

Play It Straight

Check bits for straightness before using them by slowly rolling them across a flat surface with your fingertips. The ends of the bit should not wobble. If they do, the bit is bent and should be discarded. A bent bit can break during use, causing accidents or damage to the workpiece.

Bit Block for Better Boring

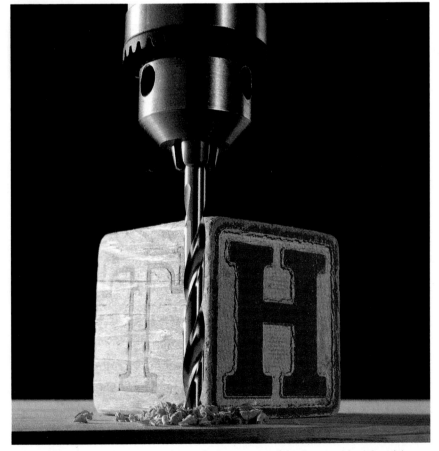

Drill perfectly straight holes by using a square block as a visual guide. Keep the drill bit shank parallel to the corner of the block when drilling.

Keep Your Temper

Drilling metal or extremely hard woods can overheat a drill bit and destroy the temper of the metal drill bit. Prevent the bit from overheating by using light machine oil to lubricate the surface you are drilling. Take care when applying machine oil to wood: use small amounts of oil to prevent staining the workpiece.

How to Sharpen Twist Bits

Sharpen twist bits made of high-speed steel with an electric bit sharpener. Twist bits have precisely curved cutting edges that are impossible to sharpen by hand. Twist bits made from metal alloys, like carbide or titanium, should be sharpened by a professional.

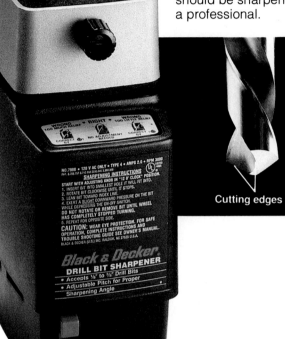

Cutting edges

How to Sharpen Sawtooth Bits

Lifter

Teeth

Throat

Sharpen each tooth with a few light strokes of a triangular saw file, filing in one direction only. Make sure the teeth are equal in height. File the lifter from the inside, passing the file through the throat of the bit.

How to Sharpen Brad-point Bits

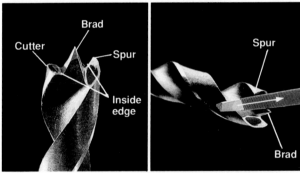

Brad

Cutter

Spur

Spur

Inside edge

Brad

A brad-point bit has a center cutting point called a brad, and a pair of cutters with outside points called spurs. Sharpen the spurs and the inside edges of the cutters with a triangular saw file. Keep the pairs of cutters and spurs at the same height, and take off as little material as possible when sharpening.

How to Sharpen Spade Bits

Wings

File upward

Wing cutters

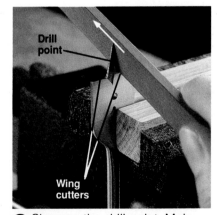

Drill point

Wing cutters

1 Clamp the bit securely in the wooden jaws of a bench vise. Grip the wings of the bit in the vise so the bit cannot rotate.

2 Sharpen the wing cutters, using a flat metal file. Maintain the angle of the wing cutters, and make a few light strokes, filing upward only. The finished surface should be shiny and smooth.

3 Sharpen the drill point. Maintain the angle of the point's cutting edge, and file in one direction only. Keep the file flat against the cutting edge, and avoid touching the wing cutters.

Tooth Guard

Protect handsaw teeth and prevent accidents by covering the cutting edge with a protective sheath when the saw is not in use. A saw sheath can be made from a narrow strip of wood, rigid foam, or old garden hose. Cut a lengthwise slot into one edge of the sheath, then fit it over the saw teeth.

Wood

Rigid foam

Garden hose

Easy Does It

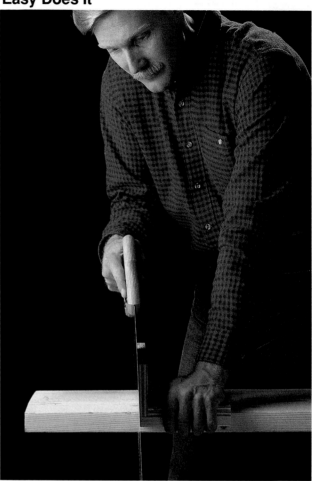

A proper stance is important for good sawing technique. Always take the time to get comfortable before sawing, and make sure your hand, elbow, and shoulder are directly in line with the saw blade. Saw with a steady rhythm, applying slight pressure on the push strokes and relaxing on the pull strokes.

Miss the Mark on Fine Work

A saw consumes from 1/16" to 1/8" of wood because of the thickness of the blade. Sawing directly on a marked cutting line may leave the workpiece slightly too small. Make cuts about 1/16" wide of the marked cutting line. Carefully plane the edge down to the line for a precise fit.

Get the Point

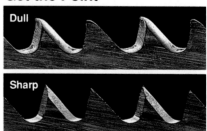

Dull

Sharp

Examine handsaws often for sharpness. On dull saws, the teeth show wear, and are visibly rounded (top). Sharp saws have pointed teeth with clean, smooth edges. Dull saws should be sharpened by a professional. Check the Yellow Pages under "Saws, Sharpening."

Straight Handsaw Cuts

It is important to keep handsaw cuts square to the face and sides of the workpiece. Make this job easier by building a squaring guide from scrap hardwood or ¾" finish plywood. Use a combination square to check each piece for squareness before assembling the guide. Join the pieces with carpenter's glue and 1¼" wallboard screws, and check the final assembly again to make sure it is square.

Adjust Your Sawing Angle

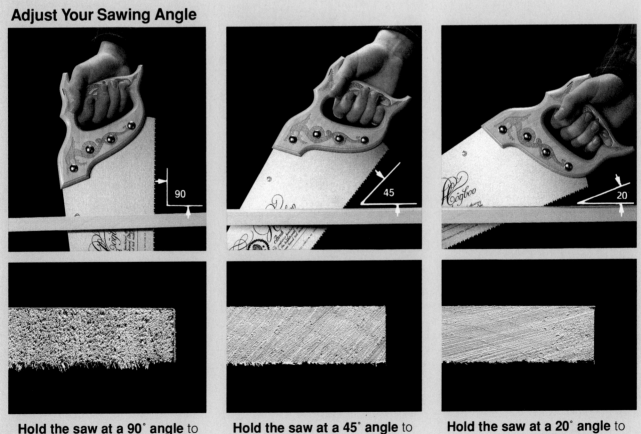

Hold the saw at a 90° angle to the workpiece to make fast cuts. This technique leaves a rough-edged cut.

Hold the saw at a 45° angle to the workpiece for most cutting jobs. This angle produces a fairly smooth cut.

Hold the saw at a 20° angle to the workpiece to make very smooth cuts. Sawing at this angle requires extra cutting time.

Keep Shaping Tools Sharp

Chisels and hand planes must be kept razor sharp to work properly. Cutting with dull chisels and planes requires excessive force, which often results in gouged workpieces and splintered wood fibers. Dull tools also can slip, causing injury.

On the Cutting Edge

Protect the sharp cutting edge of a chisel with an old tennis ball. Cut a small slit in the ball, and slip it over the tip of the chisel.

Get It Straight

Using a chisel is a fast, easy way to cut out a mortise. But keeping the edges of a deep mortised area perpendicular can be difficult. Use a square block to line up your chisel and guarantee straight mortise edges. Cut with the beveled side of the chisel held toward the inside of the mortise.

How to Chisel Properly

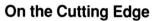

1 Score the outline of the cutting area with the chisel. Hold the beveled side of the chisel toward the inside of the marked area, and tap the butt of the chisel lightly with a mallet.

2 Make a series of parallel cuts, ¼" apart and about ¼" deep, across the marked area. Hold the chisel at a 45° angle to the workpiece, with the blade perpendicular to the wood grain.

3 Lever out the wood chips by chiseling in the opposite direction. Repeat steps 2 and 3 until cut reaches desired depth, then trim to the marked lines, making sure the edges of the cut are flat.

Sharpening Chisels & Plane Blades

It is a good idea to sharpen chisels and planes before each use — even if the tools are brand-new. The factory edges on new blades are sharpened by machine, and are not as sharp as hand-sharpened blades.

Sharpening a tool blade is a two-step process. First, the tool is rough-ground on an electric bench grinder, then it is finish-honed on a fine-grit sharpening stone. If you do not have a

bench grinder, you can use a coarse-grit sharpening stone to rough-grind the blade.

Everything You Need:

Tools: electric bench grinder or coarse-grit sharpening stone, work gloves, fine-grit sharpening stone.

Materials: cup of water, light machine oil.

How to Sharpen Chisels & Plane Blades

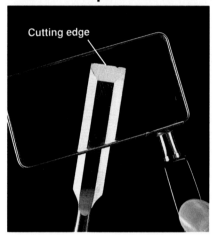

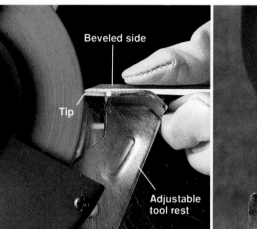

1 Inspect the cutting edge for nicks. Before the blade can be honed on a sharpening stone, any nicks in the steel must be completely removed by grinding.

2 Grind off nicks, using a bench grinder with a medium-grit wheel. Hold the tool on the flat portion of the tool rest, with the beveled side facing up. Hold the tip against the wheel and move it from side to side. Make sure the cutting edge remains square, and cool the blade frequently in water to prevent the metal from losing its temper.

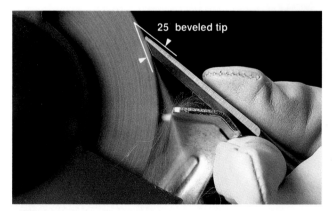

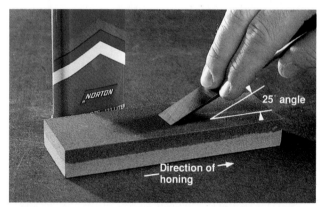

3 Rough-grind the cutting edge by turning the blade so that the beveled side is down. Rest the blade on the angled portion of the tool rest. Move the blade from side to side against the wheel to grind the tip to a 25° bevel, checking often with an angle gauge (page 49). Cool the metal frequently in water while grinding.

4 Finish-hone the cutting edge on a fine-grit sharpening stone. Place a few drops of light machine oil on the stone to lubricate the steel and to float away grit and filings. Hold the blade at a 25° angle so the bevel is flat against the stone. Draw it several times across the stone, lifting it away after each pass. Wipe the stone often with a clean rag, and apply oil after each wiping.

(continued next page)

How to Sharpen Chisels & Plane Blades (continued)

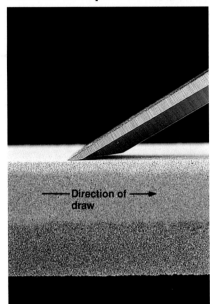

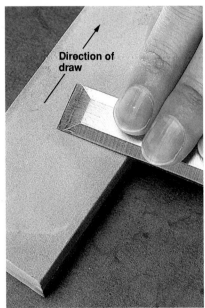

5 Put a "micro-bevel" on the blade by lifting it slightly so only the tip touches the stone. Draw blade two or three times across the stone, until a slight burr can be felt along the back of the blade.

6 Turn the blade over. Holding the blade flat, draw it across the stone one or two times to remove the burr.

7 Examine the cutting edge of the blade. The fine micro-bevel should be about 1/16" wide. This micro-bevel gives the chisel its razor-sharp edge.

Sponge Bath

One way to keep the blade cool when grinding is to hot-glue a piece of sponge to the back of the blade near the cutting edge. Dip the blade in water. The sponge holds water against the back of the blade to draw off heat. When the sponge gets warm, wet it again.

Temper, Temper

Keep a container of cool water close by when grinding a tool blade. Dip the blade in water frequently to prevent heat from ruining the temper of the steel. When the beads of water on the blade evaporate, it should be dipped again.

Make an Angle Gauge to Check Blade Bevels

For best results, keep tool blades beveled at an angle of about 25°. Sharpening to a narrower angle can make a tool blade fragile, and a wider angle can cause the tool to bite into workpieces too quickly. You can make a 25° angle gauge from a piece of 1 × 2 hardwood.

Everything You Need:

Tools: miter saw, clamp, drill with 1/8" bit, screwdriver.

Materials: 3/4" scrap wood, 1 × 2 hardwood strip (at least 12" long), #8 × 1 1/4" wood screw.

How to Make a 25° Angle Gauge

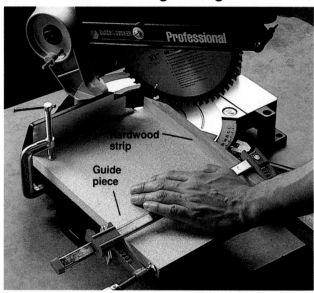

1 Clamp a squared piece of 3/4" scrap wood onto one side of the saw table as a guide piece for cutting the hardwood strip. Clamp the hardwood strip on edge against the guide piece. Set the saw blade at 25° and make the cut.

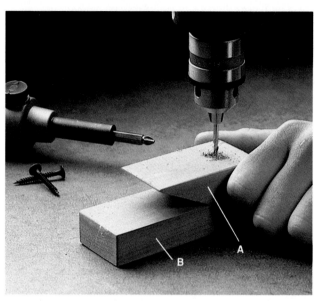

2 Cut off the beveled end so that it is about 3" long (A). Cut a second piece 6" long, with square ends (B). Place the pieces together, with the square ends flush and the bevel side down. Drill a 1/8" pilot hole and join the pieces with a #8 × 1 1/4" screw.

3 Check the bevel of the blade several times as you sharpen a chisel or plane blade. Insert the blade into the angle gauge, with the flat portion of the blade facing down (left). If the blade is beveled correctly, the tip will fit flush against both surfaces of the angle gauge (right).

Make Your Own Specialty Tools

Screwdrivers, chisels, and other ordinary hand tools can be turned into valuable specialty tools. This is a good way to make use of worn-out hand tools and save money. To create these specialty tools, all you will need is a metal file or bench grinder, and, in some cases, a propane torch.

Get the Right Angle

A right-angle screwdriver fits into tight spaces too small for an ordinary screwdriver. To make a right-angle screwdriver, clamp the tip of the screwdriver in a vise, then apply heat to the screwdriver shank with a propane torch. Apply steady pressure on the handle until the shank bends to a 90° angle.

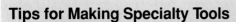

Mini Nail-puller

A small nail-puller made from an old screwdriver is useful for prying out tacks, nails, and wire brads that are too small for a hammer or pry bar. To make a mini nail-puller, bend the head of a slot screwdriver to a 30° angle, then make a V-shaped notch in the tip, using a triangular needle file.

Tips for Making Specialty Tools

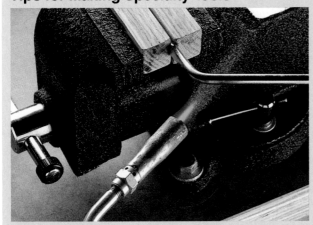

Bend tool shanks by heating them with a propane torch. Clamp the tool in a vise, then apply heat and steady pressure to bend the shank to the desired shape. Avoid excess heat: if shank becomes red-hot, the metal will lose its temper.

Reshape screwdrivers and other tools using a bench grinder (pages 47 to 48) or file. When grinding, cool the metal periodically by dipping it in water. Put the finishing touches on a homemade tool with a metal file or sharpening stone.

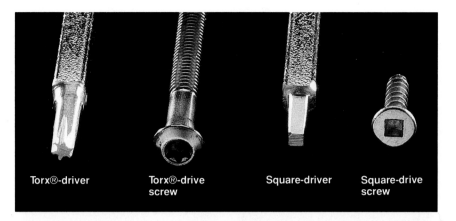

Torx®-driver   Torx®-drive   Square-driver   Square-drive
                screw   screw

Specialty Screwdrivers

Specialty screwdrivers can be made from any standard screwdriver. Make a square-driver by cutting off the head of a screwdriver with a hacksaw, then grinding four flat faces on the end of the shank. You also can make screwdrivers to fit other screw styles, such as Torx®-drive screws.

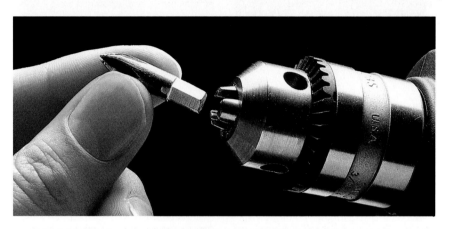

Off with Their Heads

Old screwdrivers with broken handles but good heads can be turned into screwdriver bits for your power drill. "Behead" the screwdriver with a hacksaw, then file six flat faces on the shank so that the drill chuck will grip the screwdriver bit securely.

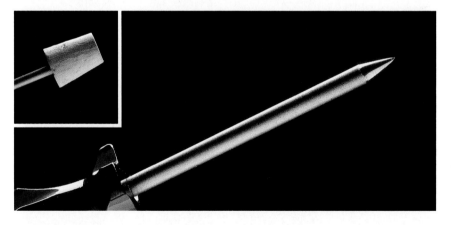

Awl You Need

Awls are useful for punching starter holes for wood screws. They also make handy scratch-markers for laying out cutting lines on wood or metal. Make your own awl by filing or grinding an ordinary screwdriver to a sharp point. When the tool is not in use, stick an old cork or tennis ball over the tip to prevent accidents.

Chiselers

A mini chisel made from a large slot screwdriver is helpful when shaping small details in wood. Bend the screwdriver shank to a 10° angle, then grind or file the screwdriver head to the desired shape. On the top face of the mini chisel, form a 25° bevel, using the same technique as for regular chisels (pages 47 to 48).

Make Your Own Woodworking Mallet

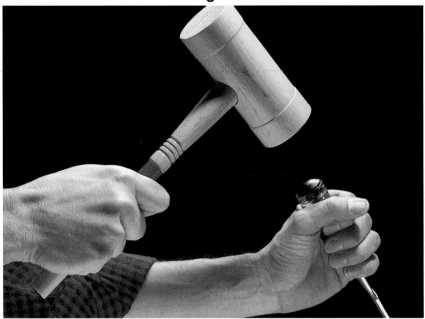

Make a woodworking mallet by cutting off the handle of an old croquet mallet. Use a mallet instead of a metal hammer when driving wood chisels or assembling wood joints. A woodworking mallet will not mar tools or workpieces.

Tool Chest Vest

A fisherman's vest makes a useful workshop "tool." The vest has many pockets of varying sizes to hold small hand tools, accessories, safety equipment, and fasteners of all sizes. If you wish, cut pieces of magnetic strips, like those found in old magnetic weatherstripping, and hot-glue them to the outside of vest pocket flaps. The magnets can be used to hold screws and nails that may be difficult to retrieve from inside a vest pocket.

Magnetic strips

Workshop Pointers

Making precise layouts requires a fine pencil point. Hot-glue an old emery board to your workbench, and use it to put a sharp tip on marking pencils.

Blade Touch-up Block

For touch-up sharpening of chisels and plane blades, keep a scrap of emery cloth attached to a wood block. Draw your blade along the block two or three times to renew the cutting edge.

Pipe Dream

Make your own pipe vise by attaching a pipe wrench to the end of your workbench. Drill mounting holes in the wrench, and anchor it to the bench with lag screws and washers.

File It Away

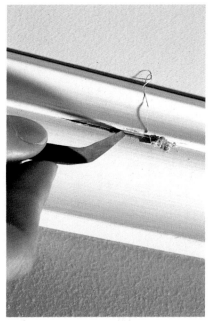

Shop files can be made into a variety of hard-working, durable specialty tools. This triangular file was ground smooth, bent to a 20° angle, and sharpened, for use as a corner paint scraper.

Mini Hacksaw

Make use of broken hacksaw blades by inserting them in a mini hacksaw handle, available at any hardware store.

Magnetize a Screwdriver

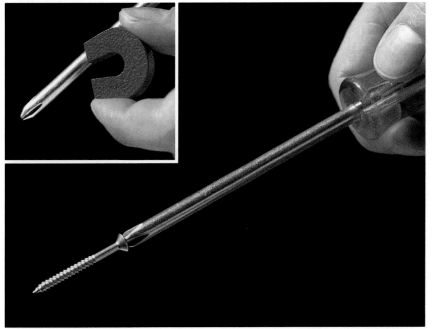

A magnetic screwdriver is handy when trying to install a screw in tight quarters. You can magnetize an ordinary screwdriver by drawing one pole of a magnet down the shaft of the screwdriver four or five times, moving in one direction only. To demagnetize the screwdriver, draw the magnet along the shaft in the opposite direction two or three times.

Double-cut Large Timbers

To cut through timbers that are thicker than the maximum blade depth of your circular saw, make matching cuts from opposite sides. Set the blade depth to slightly more than half the thickness of the lumber, and take care to keep the cuts straight.

Getting out of a Bind

Keep your saw from binding in a workpiece by driving a wood shim into the kerf after the cut is started. Keep the kerf open during long cuts by stopping the saw and moving the shim closer to the blade.

Sight Line for Sawing

Guiding a circular saw along a cutting line is easier if you draw reference marks on the front of the saw foot with a permanent marker. The cutting path for a bevel cut differs from the path for a 90° cut, so make additional reference marks for common bevel angles, like 45°.

Better Edger

An edge guide attaches to the foot of your circular saw to help it cut in a straight line. To make the edge guide more stable, attach a straight 8" strip of hardwood to the base of the guide, using pan-head screws.

Take the Plunge

Blade
guard
lever

When making plunge cuts with a circular saw, clamp a 2 × 4 on edge
onto the workpiece as a guide. Keep the edge of the saw foot up
against the 2 × 4 (inset) when lowering the blade into the workpiece.
Use two hands when making plunge cuts, and retract the blade guard
before lowering the blade.

Circular Saw Dadoes

You can use your circular saw to
cut dadoes and rabbet grooves.
Make the outside cuts first, using
a crosscut or straightedge guide
(pages 56 to 57). Then make
several parallel passes between
the outside cuts. Clean out the
material between the cuts with a
wood chisel.

Tip for Ripping

Ripping narrow boards like 2 × 4s
can be difficult and dangerous.
When making this kind of rip cut,
support the foot of the circular
saw with another board that is the
same thickness as the workpiece.

To keep the boards from sliding
as you cut, tack thin strips of wood,
like plaster lath, across the bottom of the boards to hold them in
place. Make sure tacks are away
from the cutting path of the saw.

Maintaining a Circular Saw

For smooth sawing, clean the bottom of the circular saw foot with
mineral spirits and a soft cloth
after each use. Smooth out any
burrs or scratches on the foot
with emery cloth. Polish the bottom
of the foot with auto paste wax.
Clean wood resin from the saw
blade with lacquer thinner.

This easy-to-build straightedge guide has a thin plywood base that protects workpiece surfaces and allows for easy positioning and clamping on the workpiece. Keep the metal foot of the circular saw against the cleat when cutting.

Build this Straightedge Guide to Make Long Cuts

Cut sheets of plywood or paneling quickly and accurately with this straightedge guide. Made from two plywood strips, the straightedge guide has a thin base that allows easy positioning on a workpiece. The base also keeps the foot of the circular saw from scratching workpieces.

For accurate cutting, the plywood cleat on the straightedge guide must have a perfectly straight edge. Cut the cleat on a table saw, or use a plywood strip with a factory edge that has been checked for straightness.

This project plan is designed for an 8-ft.-long straightedge guide, but you also may want to make other guides of varying lengths.

Everything You Need:

Tools: tape measure, pencil, C-clamps, circular saw.

Materials: ¼" finish plywood base (10" × 96"), ¾" plywood cleat (2" × 96"), carpenter's glue, sandpaper.

How to Build a Straightedge Guide

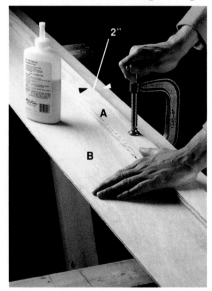

1 Apply carpenter's glue to the bottom of the ¾" plywood cleat (A), then position the cleat on the ¼" plywood base (B), 2" from one edge. Clamp the pieces together until the glue dries.

2 Position the circular saw with foot tight against the ¾" plywood cleat. Cut away excess portion of the plywood base with a single pass of the saw. Use sandpaper to smooth any rough edges.

3 To use the straightedge guide, position it with the edge of the base flush against the marked cutting line on the workpiece. Clamp the guide in place with C-clamps.

Build a Triangle Guide for Making Crosscuts & Miters

This triangle guide built from plywood scraps helps you make fast, accurate crosscuts at 90° and 45° angles. You can make additional guides for other common angles, like 30° and 60°.

For a 30°-60° guide, lay out the plywood triangle so that the sides measure exactly 12", 16", and 20". This layout, called a "3-4-5 triangle," gives precise 30°, 60°, and 90° angles.

Everything You Need:

Tools: pencil, combination square, saw.

Materials: ¾" plywood, carpenter's glue, 1¼" wallboard screws, sandpaper.

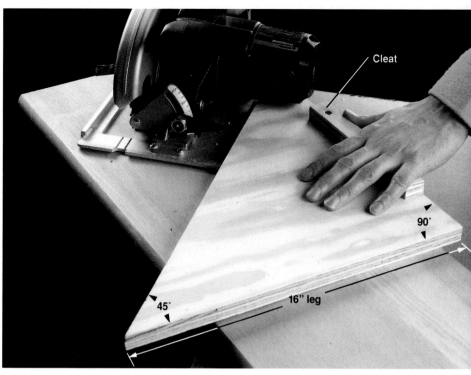

To use the crosscut guide, hold or clamp the guide so the cleat on the bottom of the guide is tight against the workpiece. Keep the foot of the circular saw firmly against the edge of the plywood triangle while cutting.

How to Make a Triangle Guide

1 Use a combination square to lay out a ¾" plywood triangle with two 45° angles and a 90° angle, and 16" legs. Cut out the triangle. Cut two ¾" plywood cleats, 8" long and 1" wide.

2 Draw a line parallel to one 16" leg of the triangle, 1" from the edge, using a combination square as a guide. Turn the triangle over, and draw an identical line on the other side.

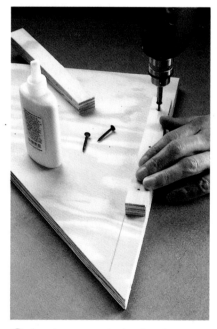

3 Apply carpenter's glue to one side of each plywood cleat. Center the cleats along the edge of the triangle, flush against the reference lines, and attach with wallboard screws. Use sandpaper to smooth rough edges.

Going around in Circles

Cut circles easily with a router, using a screw and a short length of chain. Drive the screw in the center point of the circle, then attach the end of the chain to the screw. Attach the other end of the chain to the router handle. To cut the circle, stretch the chain taut against the screw, then lower the bit into the workpiece and move the router slowly around the center point of the circle.

Stay on Edge

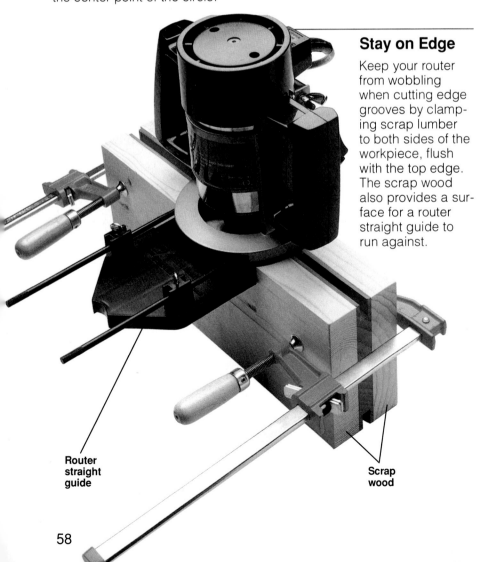

Keep your router from wobbling when cutting edge grooves by clamping scrap lumber to both sides of the workpiece, flush with the top edge. The scrap wood also provides a surface for a router straight guide to run against.

Router straight guide

Scrap wood

Stop Router Wobble

When you are cutting a decorative edge, the slightest wobble can ruin the workpiece. Keep the router base flat by clamping a piece of scrap lumber the same thickness as the workpiece to the surface of the workbench.

Homemade Router Tool

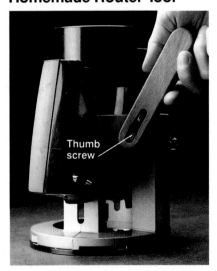

Thumb screw

Motor vibrations can tighten a router base thumbscrew so it is difficult to loosen. Make a hardwood router wrench to help loosen a stubborn thumbscrew. Cut a 1" × 5" strip of ¾" hardwood, then cut a narrow slot near one end, just large enough to slip over the thumbscrew.

Build a Router T-square for Quick, Accurate Cuts

This T-square makes it easy to cut straight grooves (dadoes) with a router. It has precut reference slots that make it easy to position the T-square accurately on the workpiece.

This plan is for a T-square with ½" and ¾" reference slots. You also can make the reference slots to match other frequently used bit sizes. If you wish, make a larger T-square for cutting grooves in sheet goods.

Everything You Need:

Tools: combination square, screwdriver, clamp, router, router bits (straight ½", ¾").

Materials: ½" plywood (3" × 18"), 2 × 4 (14" long), 1⅝" wallboard screws.

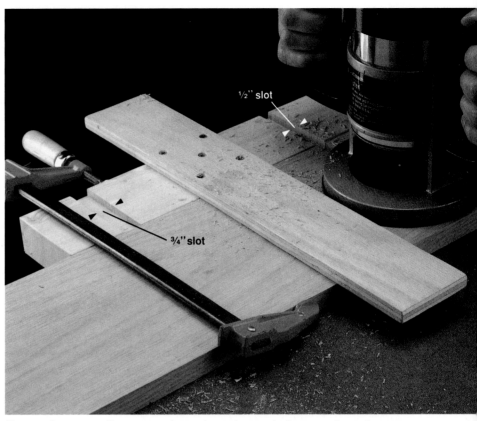

To use the router T-square, clamp it on the workpiece so the reference slot aligns with dado layout mark on the workpiece. Keep router firmly against the T-square guide arm to ensure a perfect cut.

How to Make & Use a Router T-square

1 Center one end of the guide arm (A) on the cross bar (B), so it overhangs the cross bar by 4". Use a combination square to make sure the pieces are exactly perpendicular.

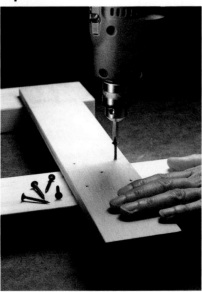

2 Attach the guide arm to the cross bar with wallboard screws. After driving the first screw, check to make sure the pieces are perpendicular, then drive the remaining screws.

3 Use your router and a ¾" straight bit to cut a ½"-deep reference slot in one side of the cross bar. Cut another slot on the other side of the cross bar, using a ½" straight bit.

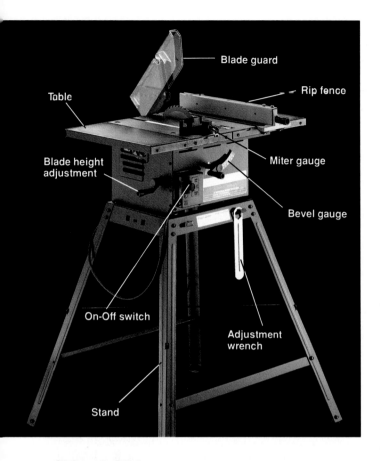

Blade guard

Rip fence

Table

Blade height adjustment

Miter gauge

Bevel gauge

On-Off switch

Adjustment wrench

Stand

The versatile table saw is the first stationary power tool purchased for many home workshops. To keep your table saw cutting safely and accurately, follow these tips:

• Always use the blade guard. Most table saw accidents occur when blade guards are not used. Although many of the photos on the following pages show the table saw with the blade guard removed, this is done for photographic clarity only. Always keep the blade guard in place when sawing.

• Use saw blades designed for the materials you are cutting (see page 72). A blade designed for cutting framing lumber usually is not suitable for fine woodworking.

• Clean away wood pitch, resin, and glue from table saw blades with an old toothbrush and lacquer thinner.

• Make your own table saw accessories to improve safety and increase the usefulness of your saw. Common, easy-to-make accessories include: pushsticks (page 63), fingerboards (pages 64 to 65), and a roller-top support stand (pages 66 to 71).

Shine & Slide

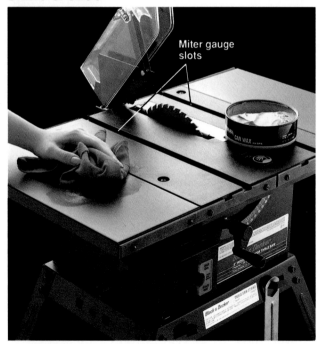

Miter gauge slots

Apply paste wax regularly to the table surface, the sides of the rip fence, and the insides of the miter gauge slots. Buff the surfaces with a soft cloth. The wax prevents rust and helps workpieces slide easily across the table surface.

Keep It Clean

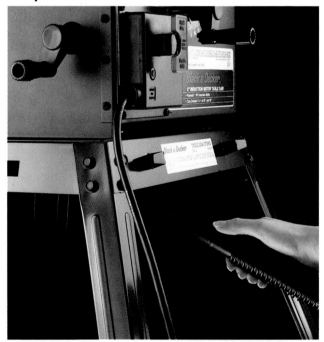

Vacuum inside the motor housing to keep the motor, adjustment screws, and pulleys free of dirt and sawdust. Sawdust buildup can cause malfunctions, such as overheating and binding.

Keep a Low Profile for Safety

Set the height of the saw blade so it extends no more than ½" above the surface of the workpiece. This minimizes the amount of exposed blade, reducing the chance of touching it accidentally as it spins. A lower blade also reduces blade friction and chipping of workpieces.

Rip Tip

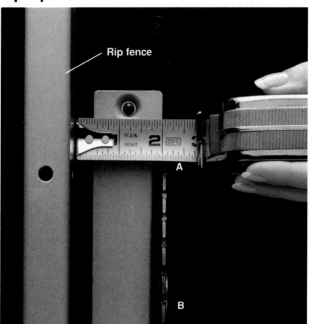

Inaccurate cuts, binding workpieces, and kickbacks are caused by a misaligned saw blade. Check the alignment of the saw blade to the rip fence before each work session. Measure the distance from the rip fence to the blade, both at the front (A) and rear (B) of the blade. Distances should be identical. If they are not, refer to your owner's manual for directions on aligning the saw blade.

Straddle the Fence

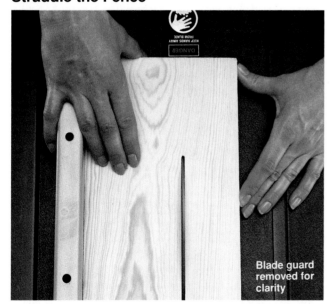

Keep your guide hand away from the blade by hooking the little finger of your hand over the rip fence while cutting. This keeps your hand from slipping off the workpiece and toward the spinning blade.

Cut Big Boards Better

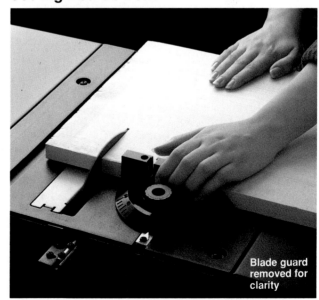

Cut boards that are too wide for the miter gauge in its normal position by turning the miter gauge around so that it precedes the board. Hold the board snugly against the miter gauge, and feed the board slowly into the blade.

How to Check the Vertical Alignment of the Blade

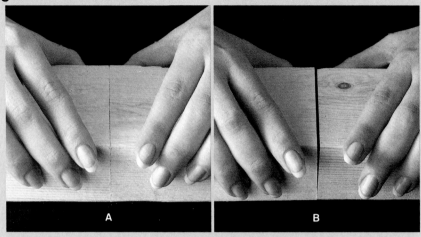

Blade guard removed for clarity

1 Set both the table saw blade and the miter gauge to 0°. Make a test crosscut on a short length of 2 × 4.

2 Put both pieces of the cut 2 × 4 on a flat surface. Turn one piece upside down, and place the cut ends together. If the ends meet perfectly (A), the blade is exactly vertical. If there is a gap between the two pieces of 2 × 4 (B), then the saw blade is not aligned correctly. Refer to the owner's manual for instructions on how to align the saw blade so it is square to the table.

Put Up a Bigger Fence

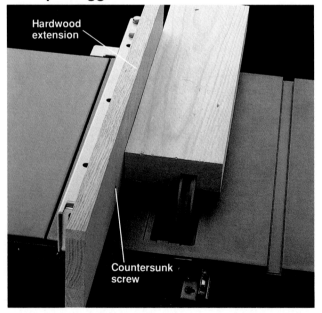

Hardwood extension

Countersunk screw

Long boards are difficult to keep straight while ripping them on the table saw. Solve this problem by attaching a hardwood extension to the rip fence. A larger fence also provides a surface for attaching a finger-board (pages 64 to 65). The hardwood extension may be any length or height, but the wood must be straight, and free of warping and cupping. Bolt the extension to the rip fence with machine screws and wing nuts, using the mounting holes predrilled on the fence. Make sure to countersink the screw heads so they do not extend past the face of the hardwood.

Miter Mate

Countersunk screws

Long boards tend to wobble during crosscutting. Solve this problem by attaching a hardwood extension to the miter gauge. The hardwood extension should be straight, and free of warping and cupping. Bolt the extension to the head of the miter gauge with machine screws and wing nuts. Make sure to countersink the screw heads so they do not extend past the face of the hardwood. Make a "right-hand" (above) and "left-hand" extension for easy crosscutting from either side of the blade.

Make a Pushstick for Safety

Blade guard removed for clarity

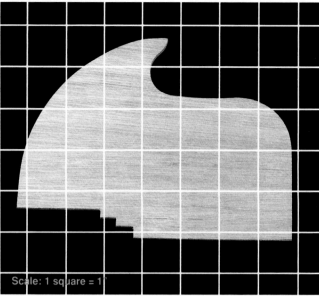

Scale: 1 square = 1"

A pushstick is a safety accessory designed to keep your fingers away from the blade as you guide a workpiece across the table saw. This pushstick has several notches to accommodate different thicknesses of wood. The notches grip the back of the workpiece as you press it down against the table and push it forward through the saw blade.

Make the pushstick from plywood dimension lumber free of knots, warping, and other defects. If you wish, make a photocopy transfer (page 88) of the pattern shown above. Make several pushsticks for a variety of ripping tasks. Narrow ¼" pushsticks are helpful when ripping thin workpieces, but wider pushsticks are more stable.

Straddle Stick Safety

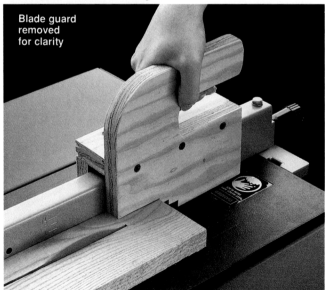

Blade guard removed for clarity

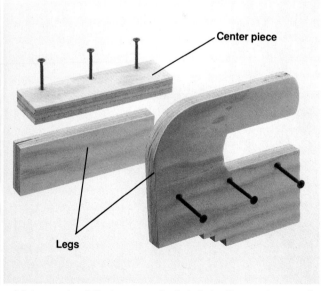

Center piece

Legs

A straddle-type pushstick has two legs that slide on each side of the rip fence. This pushstick is especially stable, preventing the operator's hand from slipping away from the fence and toward the saw blade. The handle of the straddle pushstick should always be over the workpiece. If you are cutting with the rip fence on the left side of the blade, make a "left-hand" pushstick with the handle on the right side.

Make a straddle-type pushstick from three pieces of hardwood or plywood. To prevent wobbling, size the center piece so that the gap between the legs is no more than ⅟₁₆" greater than the thickness of the rip fence. The legs ride directly on the table surface, and should be long enough that the center piece clears any adjustment bolt heads on top of the rip fence. Join the pieces with wallboard screws.

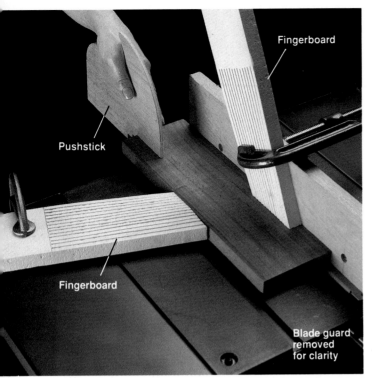

Two fingerboards clamped against the saw table and rip fence are especially helpful for making dadoes or precise cuts on hardwoods.

Use Fingerboards for Safe, Accurate Cutting

A fingerboard is an easy-to-make table saw accessory that is clamped to the rip fence or saw table to help guide a workpiece while cutting. It has springlike fingers that apply steady pressure as the workpiece is fed through the saw blade. Fingerboards are especially useful in fine woodworking projects, where the slightest error can ruin a workpiece.

Using fingerboards improves saw safety. When used properly, fingerboards reduce the chance of kickbacks; they also keep the operator's hands well away from the saw blade. When cutting narrow workpieces, use a pushstick in addition to fingerboards.

Everything You Need:

Tools: pencil, combination square, jig saw with wood-cutting blade, C-clamp.

Materials: straight-grained 1 × 4 pine lumber (about 12" long).

How to Make & Use a Fingerboard

1 Select a piece of straight-grained 1 × 4 pine lumber. The board must be free of knots, checks, or splits. Use a combination square to mark a stop line 8" from the end of the board.

2 Mark a series of parallel lines, ¼" apart, from the long end of the board to the stop line.

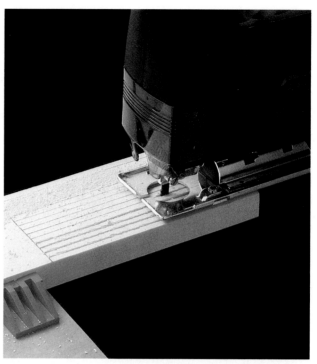

3 Make sure the wood is clamped securely on a workbench or portable work station with the marked portion overhanging the edge of the work surface. Mark the end of the board at a 20° angle, then trim off the end, using a jig saw.

4 Make a series of parallel cuts from the end of the board to the stop line, following the marked lines carefully. Stop the jig saw at the end of each cut, and allow the blade to come to a complete halt before removing it.

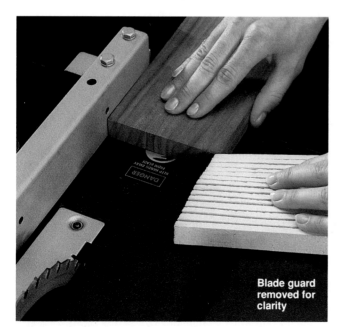

Blade guard removed for clarity

Blade guard removed for clarity

5 To use the fingerboard, place the workpiece on the saw table, about 4" in front of the blade. Position the fingerboard at an angle, slightly blocking the front corner of the workpiece. Clamp the fingerboard to the saw table with a C-clamp or handscrew. The fingerboard should be positioned so force is applied against the rip fence, not against the saw blade.

6 Turn on the saw. Feed the workpiece into the blade with steady hand pressure. The fingerboard "fingers" should flex slightly as the workpiece travels forward. Use a pushstick (page 63) to guide the workpiece past the fingerboard.

Roller-top Support Stand for Safe Sawing

A roller-top support stand helps support large materials for safe and accurate cutting on a table saw, radial arm saw, router table, or other stationary power tool. This support stand adjusts from 27" to 48" to match the height of any table saw, and has swivel casters to guide workpieces smoothly off the saw table.

The roller-top support stand can be built with scrap pieces of ¾" plywood, and requires two or three hours to construct.

Everything You Need:

Tools: saw, pencil, combination square, drill, twist bits (⁵⁄₃₂", ¼"), C-clamp, screwdriver, tape measure.

Materials: ¾" plywood, carpenter's glue, wallboard screws (1⅝", 2"), two carriage bolts (¼" × 6") with washers and wing nuts, six swivel casters (1¼"), ¾" self-drilling pan-head screws.

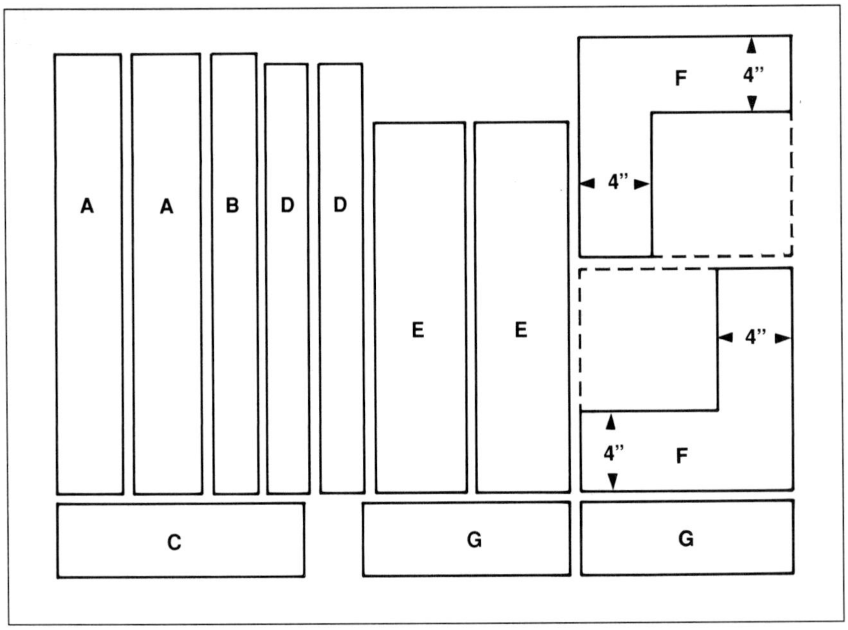

Lumber Cutting List

Key	Pcs	Description
A	2	¾" I-beam side, 4" × 24"
B	1	¾" I-beam center board, 2⅝" × 24"
C	1	¾" top, 4" × 14"
D	2	¾" guide strip, 2 ⁹⁄₁₆" × 23"
E	2	¾" side column, 5½" × 20"
F	2	¾" L-brace, 12" × 12"
G	2	¾" foot, 12" × 4"

How to Build the Support Stand I-beam

1 Set the blade of a combination square at 2", and use the square as a guide (page 86) to draw a centerline down the front of each I-beam side (A).

2 Drill four evenly spaced ⁵⁄₃₂" pilot holes along the centerline on each I-beam side.

3 Turn the I-beam sides over, and draw two reference lines on each piece to indicate where center board (B) will be attached. Locate the lines 1⁵⁄₈" from edges.

4 Apply carpenter's glue between the reference lines on one side of an I-beam side.

5 Align the center board (B) between the reference lines on one of the I-beam sides, and clamp in place. Make sure the ends of the center board are flush with the ends of the I-beam side.

6 Turn the clamped pieces over, and check to make sure the pieces are properly aligned. Drive 2" wallboard screws down through the pilot holes and into the center board.

(continued next page)

How to Build the Support Stand I-beam (continued)

7 Turn the assembled pieces over. Complete the I-beam assembly by attaching the remaining I-beam side to the center board with carpenter's glue and 2" wallboard screws.

8 On the I-beam top (C) draw two reference lines, located 1" from the long edges. On each line, measure and mark two points, located 5⅜" from ends. Drill 5⁄32" pilot holes at each point.

How to Build the Support Stand Base

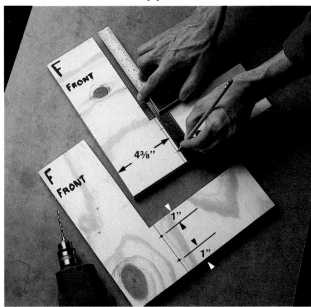

9 Apply glue to one end of the assembled I-beam. Position the I-beam top on the end of the I-beam, making sure the pilot holes are aligned with the I-beam sides. Fasten the top to the I-beam with 2" wallboard screws.

1 On each L-brace (F), label one side as the "front." With the pieces aligned the same way, draw a reference line on each L-brace, located 4⅜" from one of the long edges. On each reference line, mark two points, located 1" from the ends of the line. Drill a 5⁄32" pilot hole at each marked point.

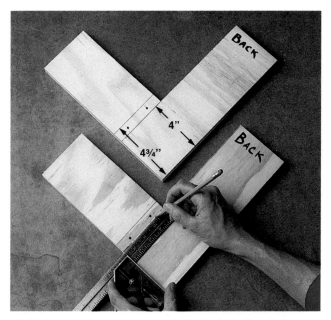

2 Turn the L-braces over, and label the "back" surfaces. On each piece, draw a pair of reference lines, located 4" and 4¾" from the long edge. The drilled pilot holes should be centered between the reference lines.

3 On each foot piece (G), draw a reference line 4⅜" from one end. On each reference line, mark two points, located about 1" from the ends of the line. Drill 5⁄32" pilot holes at each point. On each piece, draw two more lines, spaced ⅜" on either side of the first reference line.

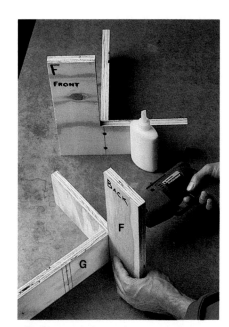

4 On each foot piece, apply a bead of carpenter's glue to the end that is closest to the pilot holes. Stand each L-brace (F) upright, then position a foot piece (G) so that the end is centered over the drilled pilot holes on the L-brace. Join the pieces with 2" wallboard screws.

5 On each foot piece, apply a bead of carpenter's glue between the reference lines drawn in step 3. Position pieces together so the edges of the L-braces are centered over the pilot holes on the foot pieces. Complete the base assembly by joining the pieces with 2" wallboard screws.

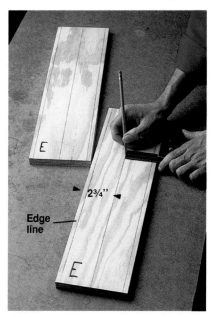

6 On each side column piece (E), draw two edge lines, located ⅜" from the edges. Draw another line down the center of each piece, located 2¾" from the edges of the side column.

(continued next page)

How to Build the Support Stand Base (continued)

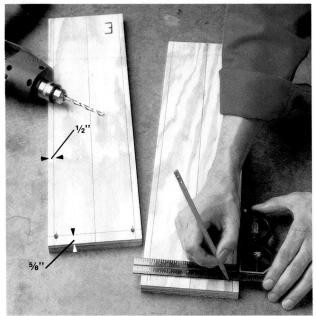

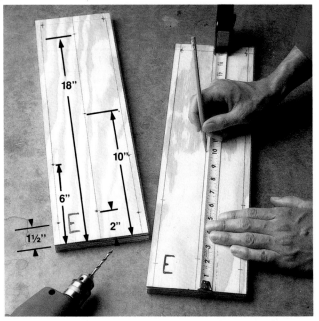

7 On each side column piece (E), draw a line across one end, located ⅝" from the end. On each line, mark two points, each located ½" from the side. Drill a ¼" pilot hole at each point.

8 From the opposite end of each side column piece, measure and mark two points along each edge line, located 1½" and 6" from the end. Along the centerline, measure and mark points at 2", 10", and 18". Drill 5/32" pilot holes at each marked point.

How to Assemble the Roller-top Support Stand

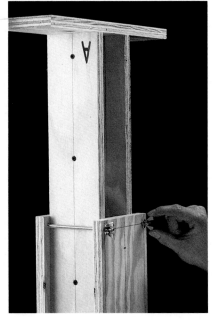

9 Attach the side columns to the base assembly, using carpenter's glue and 2" wallboard screws. The edges of the side pieces should be flush with the edges of the L-braces.

1 Insert the I-beam into the base assembly.

2 Insert carriage bolts through the pilot holes in the side columns, and loosely thread the washers and wing nuts onto the bolts. Raise the I-beam so the top is 11¾" from the top of the columns. Tighten wing nuts securely.

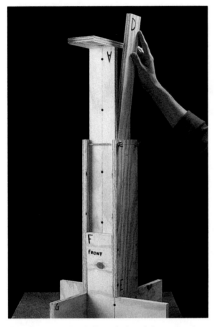

3 On each side of the I-beam, insert a guide strip (D) behind the side column.

4 Slide the guide strips down into the base assembly until the tops of the guide strips are flush with the top edges of the side columns. Fasten the guide strips to the side columns with 1⅝" wallboard screws.

5 Position six swivel casters on the support stand top, spaced evenly. Make sure the casters can swivel freely without hitting one another. Attach the casters to the support stand top with ¾" self-drilling pan-head screws.

To use the support stand, position it on the outfeed side of your table saw, about 1 ft. from the edge of the saw table. Adjust the support stand height so the tops of the casters are even with the saw table.

Mighty Miter Maker

The power miter saw is a versatile, portable tool that is especially useful for finish carpentry and woodworking projects.

When using a power miter saw, anchor it firmly with C-clamps to a workbench or portable work station. Reduce vibrations and tool noise by placing pads cut from an inner tube or carpet padding between the saw legs and the work surface. Prevent rust from forming on the saw bed by polishing it with auto paste wax.

Many shop workers increase the size of the metal saw bed by attaching a layer of ¾" particleboard or plywood over the bed. The oversized wood layer protects the metal bed and provides extra support when cutting long boards.

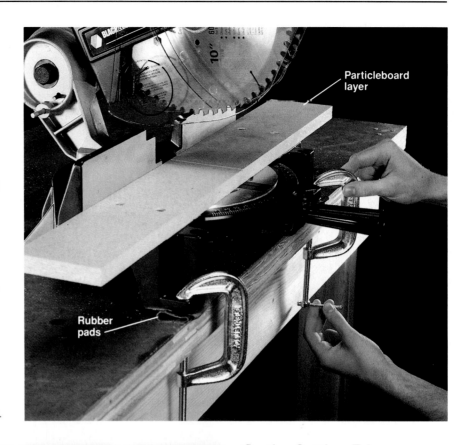

Particleboard layer

Rubber pads

On the Cutting Edge

The quality of the cut produced by a power saw depends on the type of blade you use and the speed at which the blade is forced through the workpiece. In general, let the saw motor reach full speed before cutting, and lower the saw arm slowly for the best results.

A 16-tooth carbide-tipped blade (A) cuts quickly: it is good for rough cutting of framing lumber.

A 60-tooth carbide-tipped blade (B) makes a smooth cut in both softwoods and hardwoods. It is a good all-purpose blade for general shop work.

A precision-ground crosscut and miter blade (C) makes extremely smooth, splinter-free cuts. It is an ideal blade for your fine woodworking projects.

An abrasive friction blade (D) makes fast cuts on thin steel, galvanized metals, and iron pipes.

A

B

C

D

Keep It under Lock & Key

Prevent unauthorized use of a miter saw by locking it with a small luggage padlock placed through the hole in the trigger.

Easy Angle Finder

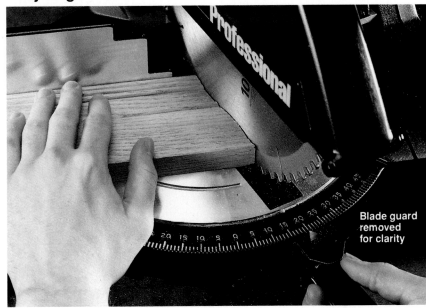

Blade guard removed for clarity

Use your miter saw as a protractor to find the angle of mitered workpieces. Lock the saw blade in the down position, then place the workpiece on the miter saw table, tight against the rear fence. Adjust the saw arm until the blade is tight against the angled portion of the workpiece. Read the miter scale to find the angle of the workpiece.

Crowning Touch

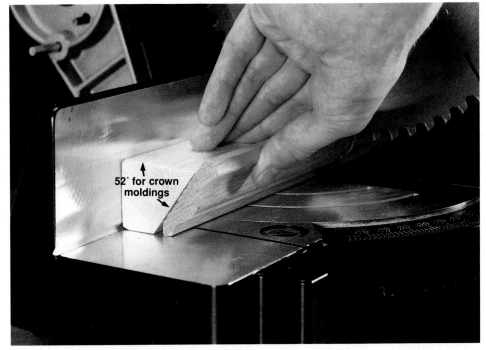

52° for crown moldings

A Square Deal

Correct blade alignment is essential for accurate mitering. Over time, a miter saw can lose its alignment. Before each job, check the alignment between the blade and the saw table, using a carpenter's square or the blade alignment test described on page 62. Realign the blade according to the directions in your owner's manual. Most power miter saws have handle bolts underneath the saw table that can be loosened to readjust the alignment of the blade.

Crown and cove moldings do not lie flat on the wall when installed. For this reason, it is difficult to miter them accurately. To make this job easier, attach a beveled spacer block to the miter saw fence to duplicate the angle at which the molding will be installed. For crown moldings, bevel the spacer block at 52°; for cove moldings, bevel the block at 45°. Drill holes through the rear of the fence, and attach the block to the fence with pan-head screws.

Blade guard removed for clarity

Maximum Mitering

A standard miter saw with a 10" blade makes a cut 5¼" long with the blade set at 90°, and 4" long with the blade set at 45°. You can cut through wider boards by placing a 2 × 4 block on the saw table. The block raises the workpiece so more of the saw blade cuts into it. With the block, the maximum cut is 6¼" at 90°, and 4½" at 45°.

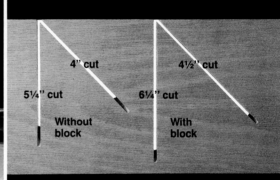

4" cut   4½" cut

5¼" cut   6¼" cut

Without block   **With block**

How to Cut Extra-wide Boards

Blade guard removed for clarity

1 Make a full downward cut. Raise the saw arm, release the trigger, and let the saw blade come to a full stop.

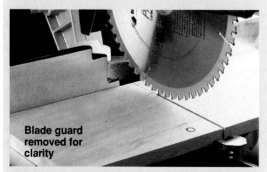

Blade guard removed for clarity

2 Turn the workpiece over, and carefully align the first cut with the saw blade. Make a second downward cut to finish the job.

Perfect Plastic Pipe Cutter

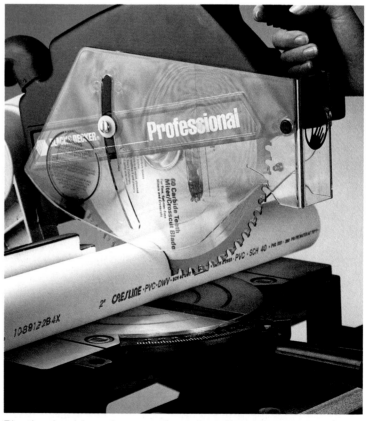

Plastic plumbing pipes can be cut easily on the power miter saw, using any type of blade. When cutting metal plumbing pipes, use an abrasive friction blade (page 72).

Prevent Kickbacks with a Miter Stop Block

When cutting many workpieces to the same length, some shop workers clamp a block of wood, called a "stop block," to the rear fence of the miter saw. They butt the workpieces against the stop block before cutting to ensure that the pieces are cut to the same size. But using a solid block of wood as a stop block can be dangerous. Small pieces of wood can jam between the saw blade and the clamped block, causing kickbacks that may injure the operator.

Avoid this danger by making this flip-out stop block from scrap 1" lumber. Size the stop block to fit your saw fence, and assemble the pieces (exploded view, right) with wire brads and carpenter's glue.

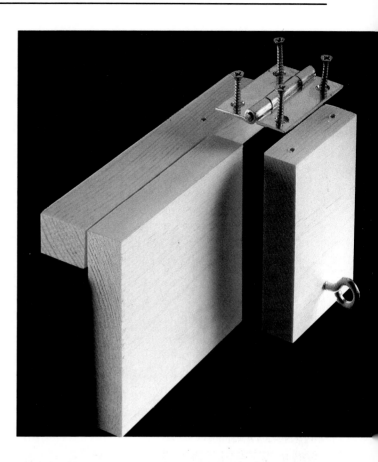

Everything You Need:

Tools: saw, screwdriver, C-clamp.

Materials: scrap 1" lumber, wire brads, carpenter's glue, 1½" × 2" hinge with screws, screw eye.

How to Use a Miter Stop Block

1 Clamp the stop block against the rear fence of the saw at the desired position, using a C-clamp. Position the workpiece on the saw bed so it butts against the stop block.

2 Hold the workpiece in place, then flip the hinged portion of the stop block out of the way. Cut the workpiece, then let the saw come to a complete stop before flipping the stop block down and cutting additional workpieces.

Build a Portable Accessory Box for Your Power Miter Saw

Build this plywood accessory box to provide extra support when cutting long workpieces on your power miter saw. When laid flat next to the saw, the box matches the height of the miter saw bed exactly. You may want to build two accessory boxes—one to provide support on each side of the miter saw.

This handy accessory box also stores extra blades and a variety of tools. You can keep tools, drill bits, pencils, and other shop items in place with strips of Velcro™ attached with small brass screws. A piece of rigid foam, shaped with a utility knife, makes a good holder for extra saw blades.

The self-centering drill bit used in this project makes accurately centered pilot holes for hinge

screws. Self-centering bits are available to fit screws from #2 to #10.

Everything You Need:

Tools: tape measure, pencil, combination square, hammer, jig saw with blades (wood- and metal-cutting), C-clamp, drill, drill bits (#2 self-centering, $5/32$" twist, $1\frac{1}{4}$" spade), power screwdriver.

Materials: $\frac{1}{2}$" finish plywood (24" × 36"), $\frac{3}{4}$" plywood ($1^{15}/_{16}$" × 24"), carpenter's glue, 4d finish nails, continuous hinge ($1\frac{1}{16}$" wide and at least 24" long, with screws), masking tape, two #8 duplex nails.

Lumber Cutting List

Key	Pcs	Description
A	1	¾" back , 1¹⁵⁄₁₆" (W*) × 24" (L)
B	1	½" bottom, 11½" (W) × 24" (L)
C	1	½" front, 2⅛" (W*) × 24" (L)
D	2	½" sides, 3⅛" (W*) × 11¾" (L)
E	1	½" top, 13½" (W) × 23⅞" (L)

Make sure plywood used for parts B, C, D, and E is exactly ½" thick. Because of manufacturing differences, some plywood sold as ½" stock actually is only ⁷⁄₁₆" or ¹⁵⁄₃₂" thick.

*This accessory box design is for the power miter saw shown on the opposite page, which has a bed height of 3⅛". Before cutting the pieces for the accessory box, measure the height of your miter saw bed with a combination square. If your saw is not 3⅛" high, adjust the width measurement (W) of pieces A, C, and D as indicated below:

Width of A = height of saw bed minus 1³⁄₁₆"
Width of C = height of saw bed minus 1"
Width of D = height of saw bed

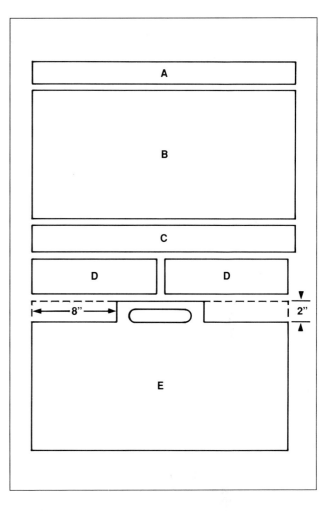

How to Make a Power Miter Saw Accessory Box

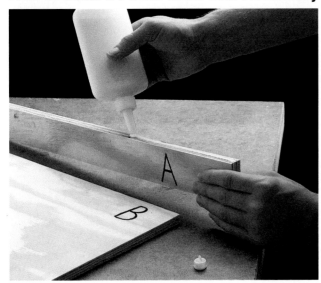

1 Apply carpenter's glue to one of the long edges of the back piece (A).

2 Position the bottom (B) over the glued edge of the back (A). Make sure all edges are flush. Nail the bottom to the back with 4d finish nails. Support the bottom with scrap wood to hold it level while nailing.

(continued next page)

How to Make a Power Miter Saw Accessory Box (continued)

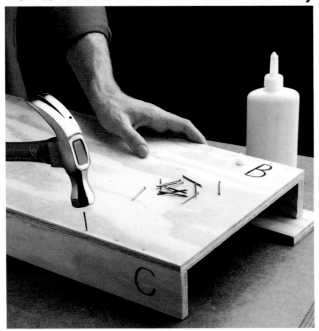

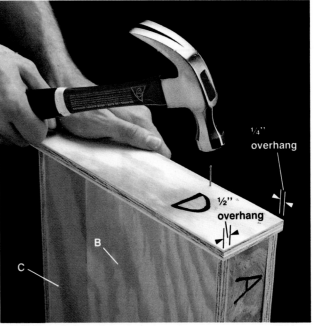

3 Apply carpenter's glue to one of the long edges of the front (C). Position the bottom (B) over the front, making sure all edges are flush. Attach the bottom to the front with 4d finish nails.

4 Stand box upright on one end. Apply carpenter's glue to all edges of the exposed end. Position a side (D) so edges are flush with the front (C) and the bottom (B). The side should overhang by ¼" at the back of the box (A) and by ½" at the top. Attach the side piece with 4d finish nails. Turn the assembly over and attach the other side piece.

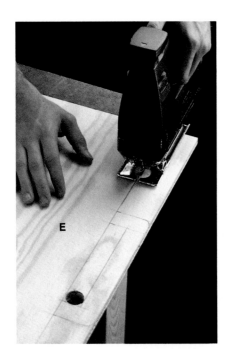

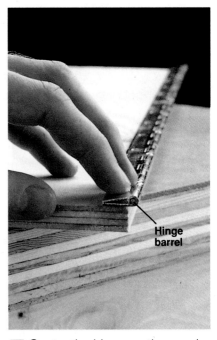

5 Draw the handle outline on the top (E). Start the cutout for the handle by drilling a 1¼" pilot hole, then finish the cutout with a jig saw.

6 Trim the continuous hinge to 23⅞" with a jig saw. To keep vibrations from ruining the cut, clamp the hinge as close as possible to the cutting line.

7 Center the hinge on the rear inside edge of the top (E) so the hinge barrel lies along the edge. Open the hinge and tape it in place with masking tape.

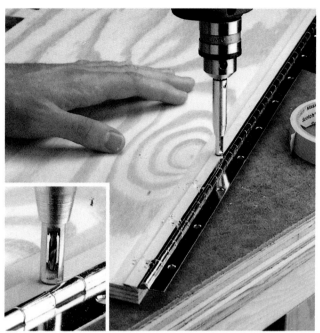

8 Locate the hinge screw holes through the tape. Use a #2 self-centering bit (inset) to drill pilot holes down through the tape and into the top. Attach the continuous hinge to the top with the hinge screws. Peel away the tape.

9 Position the top (E) against the back of the box (A) so that the edge of the hinge is ⅛" from the edge of the back. Drill pilot holes down through the hinge holes and into the edge of the back, using a self-centering bit. Attach the continuous hinge with the hinge screws.

10 Close the box. On each side (D), mark a point ¼" from the top and ½" from the front. At each point, drill a 5⁄32" hole through the side and into the edge of the top (E). Insert a duplex nail into each hole to keep the box closed when carrying it.

Customize the inside of the box to provide storage for tools and accessories. Attach Velcro™ strips with small brass screws to hold drill bits, and hand tools.

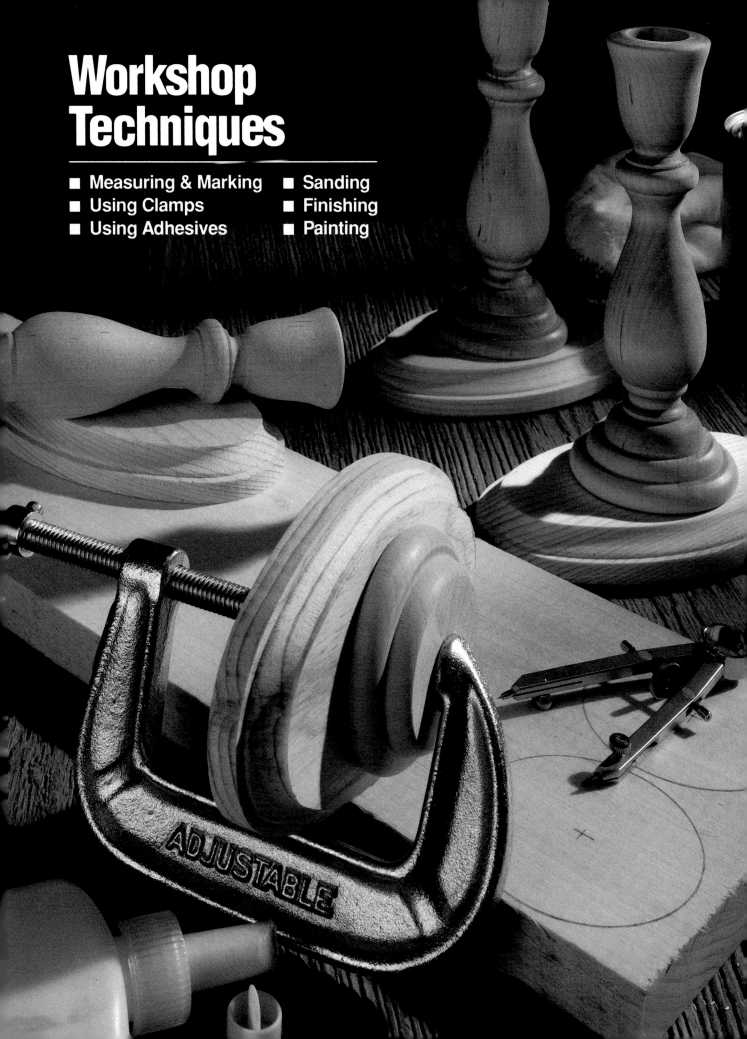

Workshop Techniques

- Measuring & Marking
- Using Clamps
- Using Adhesives
- Sanding
- Finishing
- Painting

Using good tools and materials is just part of what goes into making a successful project. In particular, the basic techniques used to begin and complete a project affect its attractiveness, and the ease and accuracy of your work.

This section presents dozens of tips and innovations that will help you improve these techniques. Not only will these tips give you better results, they will save you time and money.

Included are tips that help you begin a project with precise patterns, and show you more accurate measuring methods. Other tips show you more effective clamping techniques, and how to get the best use from adhesives. Finally, there are more tips for sanding, and for finishing or painting your workpiece.

Standard Circles

A piece of shelving standard makes a quick and versatile compass. Drive a nail through the screw hole at one end of the standard and into the workpiece to mark the center of the circle. Place the pencil in one of the slots so that the distance between the nail and the pencil is equal to the radius of the circle. Rotate the standard around the nail to draw the circle.

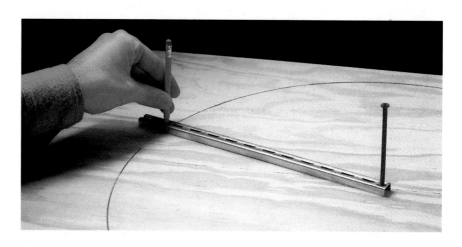

Quick Rough-cut Marking

Use your finger and a pencil to make quick, "close-enough" marks for rough cuts. Hold the pencil between your thumb and forefinger as shown. The width you wish to mark determines how far from the tip you must hold the pencil. Brace the last three fingers against the edge of the board and use them to guide the pencil as you pull it toward you.

Separate & Not Equal

Different tape measures do not always measure equally. A slight difference in the end hooks can create an error of 1/16" or more between two tapes, even if they are the same brand and style. If possible, use only one tape measure while working on a project. If you must work with two tapes, check them to make sure they record the same measurement.

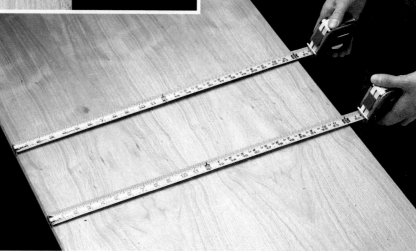

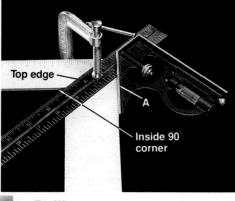

Top edge

A

Inside 90°
corner

Bull's-eye

Find the center of a round or cylindrical workpiece with this jig. Clamp a combination square onto a framing square (above) so that the 45° face of the combination square (A) rests against one leg of the framing square. The top edge of the combination square should intersect the inside 90° corner of the framing square.

Place the jig over the workpiece so both legs of the framing square touch the edges of the workpiece, as shown (left). Draw a pencil line along the top edge of the combination square blade. Rotate the workpiece several times and mark additional lines. The center of the workpiece is the point where the lines intersect.

Accurate Inside Measurements

Taking an accurate inside measurement of a drawer or box is difficult because a tape measure blade will not fit into a corner (left). The measurement on the tape measure case that indicates its length is not accurate enough for precise work. For accurate measurements, position a square in the bottom of the workpiece, tight against the corner (below). Use a tape measure to measure from the opposite side of the workpiece to the tip of the square. Add the length of the square blade (A) to the tape measurement (B) to find the total inside measurement.

Skip the Hook

The end hook on a tape measure has a small amount of play in it, and should not be used when an extremely accurate measurement is needed. For precise measurements, use the 1" mark as a beginning point. Remember to subtract 1" from the final reading.

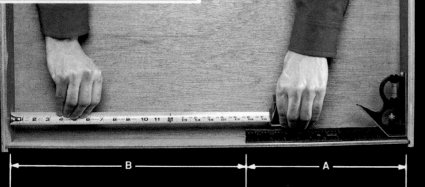

B   A

Large Circle Compass

You can make a simple compass for marking large circles using a 2"-wide strip of ½"-thick plywood. Cut the strip 2" longer than the radius of the circle. Drill a ¼" hole in the center of the strip, 1" from one end. At the other end, drill a 5/16" hole in the center of the strip, 1" from the end. Push the point of an awl through the ¼" hole and into the workpiece at the center of the circle. Insert a pencil into the 5/16" hole, and keeping the pencil straight up and down, rotate the strip around the awl to mark the circle.

Long Division

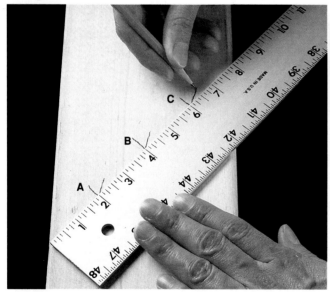

Dividing a board lengthwise into equal strips is difficult if the width of the board is not easily divisible by the number of parts. For example, you want to cut a 5¾"-wide board into 4 equal strips. To do this job quickly and easily, position the 0" end of a ruler at one edge of the board. Angle the ruler across the board until the opposite edge of the board touches an inch measurement that is easily divisible by the number of parts. For the example above, the ruler is angled until the 8" mark touches the edge of the board, and 8" divided by 4 equals 2". Mark the board at this interval along the ruler (A, B, C). Repeat this procedure at another location on the board, then use the marks to draw parallel cutting lines on the board.

Multi-digital Leveling

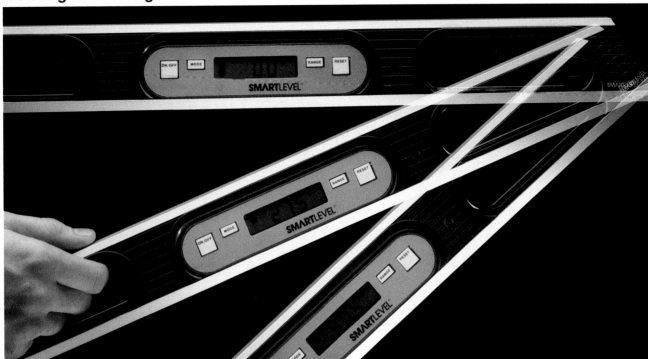

Electronic levels are new tools providing very accurate angle readings with digital readouts instead of bubble gauges. They will also measure pitch and slope percentages automatically. Powered by a replaceable battery, electronic levels are very durable and are easy to recalibrate. The electronic components are contained in a module that can be used alone as a torpedo level, or inserted into frames of varying lengths.

Is Your Level on the Level?

A
Level is color coded for clarity

B

Check a level frequently to ensure that it reads correctly. Before buying a new level, check to make sure it is accurate. To check a level for accuracy, hold one side of the level against an even surface (A), and read the bubble gauge carefully, noting exactly where the bubble is located against the guidelines. Turn the level 180° (B) and read the gauge again. Next, turn the level upside down and read the gauge. The bubble should be in the same position for all three readings. If not, use the mounting screws to adjust the bubble gauges until the level reads accurately. Gauges that are cracked should be replaced. If the gauges cannot be adjusted or replaced, buy a new level.

Sound Out Your Room

A sonic measuring tool, available at home centers, is a quick method for determining room size. This tool measures distance by bouncing sound waves off of hard surfaces, and units are available that will measure up to 250 feet with 99.5 percent accuracy. The tool also has a built-in calculator for adding distances and computing area and volume measurements. Temperature changes can affect the tool's accuracy, so let it adjust to room temperature for 15 minutes before using it.

Quick Check for Square

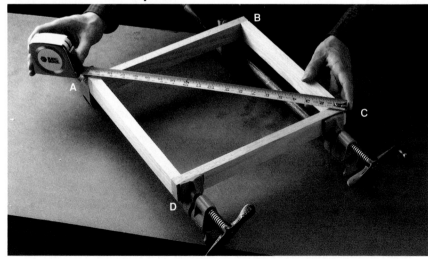

Checking for square is crucial when building frames, boxes, cabinets, drawers, and other projects where fit is important. To check for square quickly, measure the diagonals of the workpiece (A-C, B-D). The measurements will be identical if the workpiece is square.

Leveling Around Warps

Dimension lumber with slight warps and bows is usable, but checking the boards for plumb or level is difficult. Make a leveling jig for warped lumber by cutting a straightedge on a table saw, and attaching short 2 x 4 blocks to the ends. The straightedge should be slightly shorter than the lumber you are checking. Tape or clamp a level to the straightedge on the side opposite the 2 x 4 blocks. Hold the straightedge against the lumber and read the level to check for plumb or level. You can straighten the warp or bow with a cripple.

Quick Draw

To draw a line parallel to the edge of a board quickly, set the blade of a combination square to the desired distance. Position the flat side of the square against the edge of the board, and place a pencil at the end of the blade. Pull the square and pencil toward you to draw the line.

Tracing Tool

A pattern tracing wheel used in sewing also can be used to copy patterns in the workshop. Tape your pattern onto the workpiece, then follow the lines with the pattern wheel, applying downward pressure to the tool. The serrated edge of the wheel will leave marks to follow when cutting out the workpiece.

Story Pole

When marking an identical series of measurements on many workpieces, save time and improve accuracy by creating a marking pattern, called a story pole. Make the story pole from a piece of scrap lumber. Carefully mark the measurements on the story pole, then use it as a template for marking the workpieces instead of taking individual measurements.

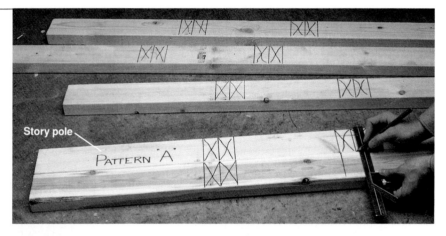

Repetitive Cuts

When you are cutting a series of identical workpieces, use only one piece as the pattern for laying out the other pieces. If you use each new piece to lay out the next piece, each new piece will be slightly larger than the last.

Diameter Gauge

To measure the diameter of round workpieces easily, make a simple gauge with a ruler and two squared blocks of wood. To find the diameter, place the workpiece between the two wood blocks and the ruler as shown. The diameter measurement is then read on the ruler. For this gauge to work properly, all six faces of each wood block must be squared.

Pattern Rubbing

To make a pattern of an object or shape that cannot be traced or photocopied, lay a sheet of white paper over the original. Rub the paper with your fingers until the features of the original make an impression in the paper. Cut out this pattern or transfer it to the workpiece with a pattern tracing wheel (page opposite).

Board Center Marker

Find and mark the center of your workpieces quickly with this simple marking jig. Make it from 2 × 4 stock and 5/16" doweling. On one side of the gauge shown here the dowels are centered 1" on either side of the pencil hole. Make sure the distance between each dowel and the pencil hole is equal. This side is used for marking center on pieces up to 1⅝" wide. The other side has the dowels centered 4⅛" on each side of the pencil hole, and is used on boards up to 7¾" wide. If you often use wider stock, you may wish to make a larger gauge.

The pattern lines from a photocopy can be transferred to a workpiece using a hot iron. It may take two or three passes with the iron to completely transfer the pattern.

Photocopy Pattern Transfer

To transfer a project pattern to a workpiece quickly and accurately, make a photocopy of the pattern and use an iron to transfer the outline to the workpiece. To make enlarged or reduced patterns, use a copying machine that has a zoom feature.

If the pattern includes any lettering, the image must be reversed before it can be transferred to the workpiece. To reverse the pattern, first make a photocopy on transparent tissue paper. Next, position the tissue copy on the photocopy machine so that the image is face up, and make a second photocopy. The second copy will have a reversed image that will transfer correctly to the workpiece.

Everything You Need:

Tools: copy machine, iron.

Materials: masking tape.

How to Make a Photocopy Pattern Transfer

1 Make a photocopy of the pattern. If possible, set the copy machine to make a dark copy. This will make transferring the copy easier.

2 Position the copy on the workpiece. Tape the copy in place, taping along one edge only.

3 Apply heat with an iron. Keep the iron moving to avoid scorching the pattern. Periodically lift the paper to check for areas that need more heat.

Contact Paper Pattern

Protect workpiece surfaces from pencil marks and scratches by covering the workpiece with clear contact paper before marking the cutting pattern. Contact paper works well on hard-to-mark surfaces, like metal and glass. Leave the paper in place until all cutting is completed.

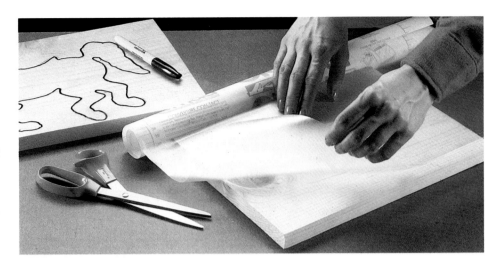

Tape Drawing Surface

Some materials, like plastic, glass, ceramics, and metals, are difficult to mark. Solve this problem by using artist's tape to provide a surface on which to draw the pattern lines. Leave the tape in place until you are finished cutting. Artist's tape is easy to remove, and can be purchased at stationery stores or art supply shops.

Marking Protrusions

Cutting around protrusions like electrical boxes can be difficult when installing paneling or other sheet goods. Simplify this job by coating the edges of the box with carpenter's chalk. Press the back side of the paneling against the box to transfer the chalk outline. Cut out the outline with a jig saw.

Drawing an Ellipse

An ellipse (or oval) often is used in the design of picture frames, table tops, custom boxes, mirror frames, and other similar projects. However, drawing a perfectly symmetrical ellipse by hand is difficult to do if you do not have a pattern to use as a guide.

The following steps show you a simple method for drawing a symmetrical ellipse onto a workpiece. This technique will work for any length and width combination your project may require.

If you do not have a compass, or if your compass does not extend far enough to use in drawing your ellipse, you can create a compass out of materials in your shop (pages 81 and 83).

Everything You Need:

Tools: straightedge, pencil, framing square, compass.

Materials: workpiece, pushpins, string.

How to Draw an Ellipse

1 Establish the length of the ellipse on a line drawn down the middle of the workpiece. The distance between points A and B equals the length of the ellipse.

2 Establish the width of the ellipse by using a framing square to draw a perpendicular line through center point C of line A-B. The distance between points D and E should be equal to the width of the ellipse and centered on point C.

3 Set the compass for the distance A-C. If you do not have a large enough compass, make one out of shop materials (pages 81 and 83).

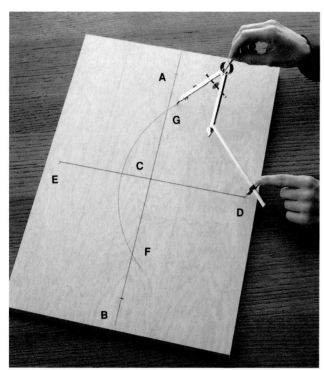

4 Position the tip of the compass at point D, and draw an arc that intersects line A-B at two points. Label these points F and G.

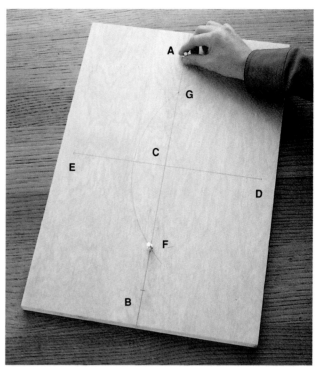

5 Insert pushpins at points F and A.

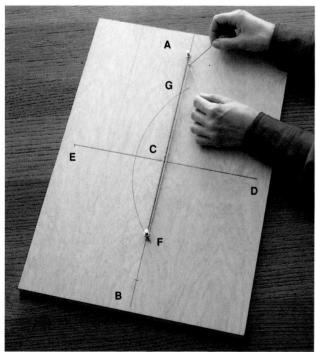

6 Loop a piece of string around the pushpins and pull it tight. Tie a knot in the string, making sure the string remains taut.

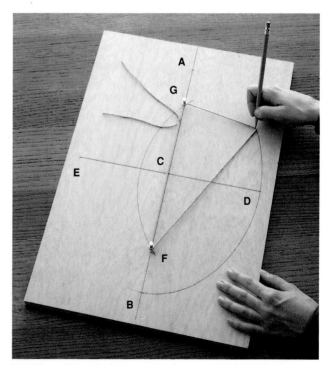

7 Move the pin from point A to point G. Put a pencil inside the loop and stretch the string against the pins. Keeping the string taut, move the pencil around the inside of the string to draw the ellipse.

Rubber Band Clamp

Use a bicycle inner tube to hold chair legs together while glued joints are drying. Loop the inner tube around the legs, and use a strip of wood to twist the rubber until it is stretched tight. Tie the strip to the inner tube to keep it from unwinding.

C-clamp Extender

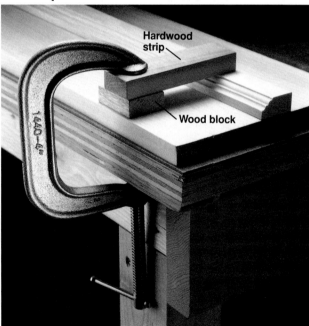

Hardwood strip

Wood block

When gluing wood trim to a flat workpiece, you can extend the reach of a C-clamp by using a short strip of scrap hardwood, and a small wood block that is the same thickness as the wood trim. Place the block close to the workpiece edge, then position the strip so it bridges the space between the block and the wood trim. Apply pressure to the strip with a C-clamp to hold the wood trim in place.

Sawhorse Stirrup

Long workpieces balanced on a pair of sawhorses can be difficult to hold in place. Hold them securely with a bicycle inner tube. Slide the inner tube over the workpiece, and use your foot to stretch the inner tube and hold the lumber in place while you work.

Gentle Jaws

Use a clothespin with the spring removed to clamp small, cylindrical items, like wooden dowels or plumbing tubes, in a bench vise. Small objects are hard to hold and can be damaged easily if clamped against the bare jaws of a vise.

Jumper Jaws

The alligator jaws from an old set of battery jumper cables make good general-purpose spring clamps. For example, use jaw clamps to hold small objects for spray painting. If needed, you can line the jaws with scraps of rubber inner tube to prevent damage to workpieces.

Cord Clamps

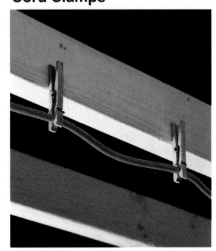

Keep electrical extension cords out of the way by clamping them in clothespins. Attach the clothespins to workshop walls and ceiling with screws or hot glue.

Spring-loaded Pliers

Turn an ordinary pliers into a spring clamp by tying a strip of rubber cut from an inner tube around the handles. Pad the jaws of the pliers with scraps of inner tube to prevent scratching a workpiece.

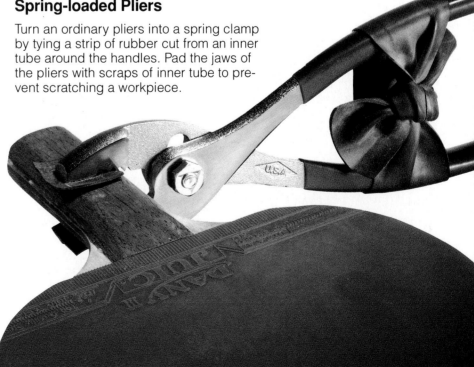

Tourniquet Clamp

Make a quick tourniquet clamp by tying a rope or nylon stocking around a workpiece. Use a screwdriver or stick to twist the rope until the loop tightens. Pad sharp workpiece corners with cardboard or rubber to protect the corners and prevent the rope from being cut. Tie the screwdriver to keep the rope from unwinding.

Long-distance Clamping

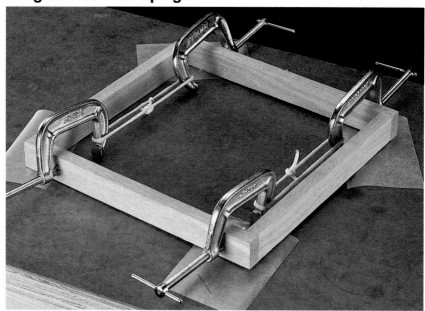

Use pairs of C-clamps to make extra-large clamps for holding frames while the glue dries. Tie a short piece of rope in a loop, then hook the stationary jaws of the C-clamps around the rope. Tighten the C-clamps to secure the workpiece.

Protective Pads for Clamp Jaws

Protect workpiece surfaces when using C-clamps by padding the metal jaws. Use a hot glue gun to attach protective pads made from felt, plastic caps from film canisters, or small scraps of wood.

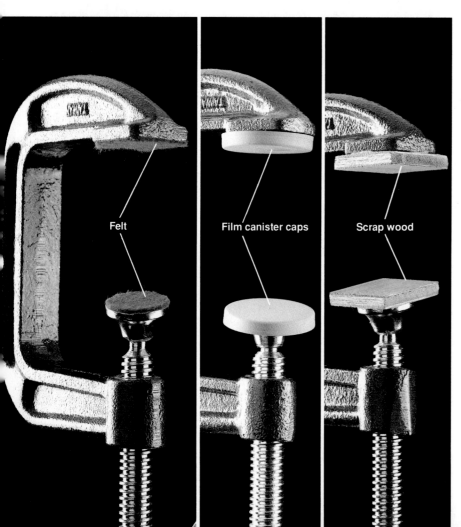

Felt

Film canister caps

Scrap wood

Pad Your Pliers

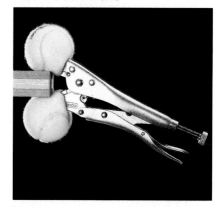

Make a temporary "soft" clamp from a pair of locking pliers. Cut slits in two old tennis balls and slide them over the plier jaws. The cloth-covered rubber protects workpiece surfaces.

Woodworker's Bench Vise

Line the jaws of a bench vise with wooden pads to prevent damage to workpieces. Each vise pad is made from two pieces of scrap plywood, and is oversized to provide better clamping. Use a jig saw to cut the frame (A) to match the shape of the vise jaws. Attach the frame to the pad faces (B) with carpenter's glue and brads.

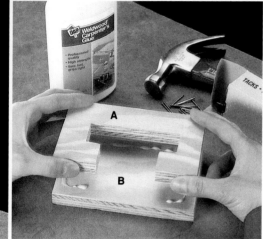

Iron-clad Clamping

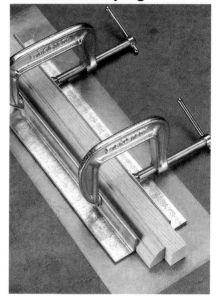

Distribute pressure and prevent bowing when clamping small pieces of wood by using two sections of angle iron and a pair of C-clamps. Angle irons also prevent clamps from damaging the wood.

True Grit for a Tight Grip

Get a better grip on smooth objects, like metal pipes, by gluing emery boards to the faces of vise jaws. The emery boards can be removed easily with a chisel or paint scraper when they are no longer needed.

Paired Pipe Clamps

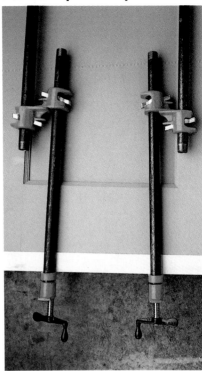

Double up two pipe clamps to grip a long workpiece. Position the clamps so the top jaws overlap, then tighten the clamps to secure the workpiece.

Highly Irregular

Irregularly shaped, delicate workpieces are difficult to grip with clamps. To hold pieces in place while glue dries, fill a plastic bag with sand and drape it over the workpiece. Sandbags of different sizes make handy hold-down aids in the workshop.

On a Pedestal

Pipe clamps and bar clamps are awkward to use when laid on a workbench. Mounting the clamps on 2 × 4 pedestals makes it easier to operate the clamp handles and provides better stability for a workpiece. Cut slots in the 2 × 4s to help keep the clamps aligned.

Clamp Power Tools in Place for Stationary Work

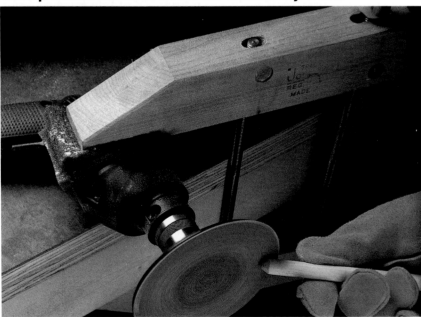

Hand power tools, like drills and sanders, can be anchored temporarily to a workbench with handscrew clamps. This technique is good for sanding small workpieces. Clamp the tool securely so it does not move, but do not damage the tool by overtightening the handscrew. A pad of soft foam or rubber under the handscrew jaw will help grip the tool while preventing damage to the tool casing.

C-clamp Miter Mate

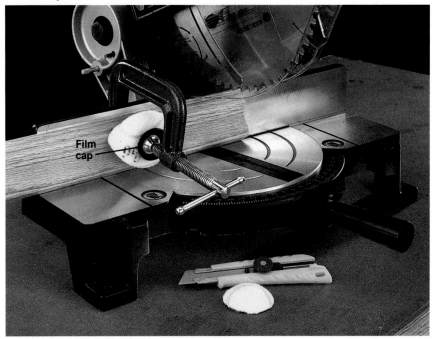

Film cap

For accurate mitering of decorative moldings, the wood must be clamped securely in the miter saw. However, ordinary clamps can damage the contours of wood moldings. Make a simple miter clamp using a C-clamp, an old tennis ball, and a plastic cap from a film canister. Cut a small slice from the side of the tennis ball, then hot-glue the film cap to the side opposite the slice, as shown above. When the miter clamp is attached to the miter saw, the soft rubber tennis ball holds the workpiece tightly without damaging the wood, and the plastic film cap keeps the C-clamp pad from slipping.

Upright Support

When painting or cutting plywood or paneling, you can support the sheet in an upright position by attaching a pair of pipe clamps to one edge, with the pipes facing in opposite directions. This technique also can be used to hold a door when drilling for locks, chiseling mortises, or planing an edge.

Rope Wrap

Make a quick rope clamp with a length of ½" nylon rope and a handscrew clamp. To use the clamp, close the back end of the handscrew around the ends of the rope. Wrap the rope around the workpiece, then tighten both clamp handles at the same time until the rope is taut.

Handy Handle

Keep a pipe clamp handy by using it as the handle for your wooden toolbox. The pipe clamp can be removed whenever you need to use it.

Door Support

These simple door clamps made from scrap lumber provide an easy way to hold doors in an upright position while installing locksets or hinges, or when planing an edge. The weight of the door causes the clamp to bend slightly and grip the sides of the door.

Each clamp requires two 2 × 4 uprights (A), 8" long; a ½" plywood cross member (B), 1½" × 16"; and two 2 × 4 foot pieces (C), 2½" long.

Join the pieces with carpenter's glue and wallboard screws. Space the uprights so the gap between them is equal to the thickness of the door. This design can be adapted to build clamps for holding framed storm windows or screens, plywood, and other sheet goods.

Vise-mounted Pipe Clamp

Decorative spindles and other long, slender workpieces can be end-clamped for sanding and finishing, using a pipe clamp secured inside a bench vise. To prevent the pipe clamp from slipping in the metal vise jaws, make a pipe holder from a pair of short, scrap 2 × 4s.

To make the pipe holder, clamp the 2 × 4s in the bench vise, then drill a hole along the seam between the boards. You may need a bit extender to make this hole. The diameter of the hole should be slightly less than the outside diameter of the pipe clamp.

Band Together

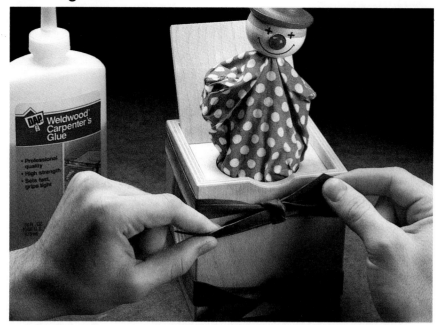

Make simple, inexpensive band clamps by cutting rubber strips from inner tubes. Wrap the strips around the workpiece and knot the ends. For greater holding power, increase the number of bands tied around the workpiece. Band clamps made from rubber will not damage workpiece surfaces or stick to wood glue.

Rope Tricks

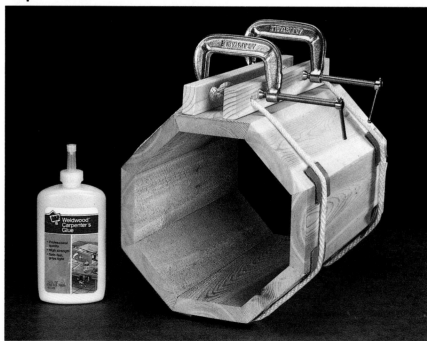

Clamp cylindrical workpieces with a double rope clamp made from a pair of 1 × 2s and two pieces of ½" nylon rope. Drill ⅝" holes near the ends of each 1 × 2, then thread the ropes through the holes and knot them. Place the double rope clamp around the workpiece, and tighten it by using C-clamps or handscrews to pull the 1 × 2s together.

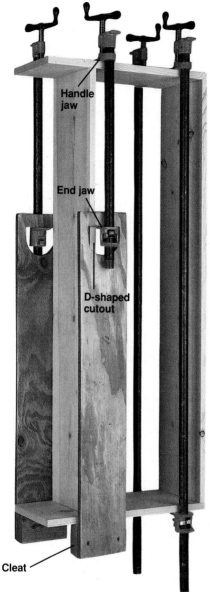

Pipe-clamp Extender

If you do not have enough long pipe clamps, you can make pipe clamp extenders from scrap strips of ¾" plywood and short 2 × 4s.

Add a D-shaped cutout to the end of each plywood strip, then attach a 2 × 4 cleat to the opposite end, as shown above.

To use the extender, hook the 2 × 4 cleat over one end of the workpiece. Position the pipe clamp with the end jaw inside the cutout, and the handle jaw over the opposite end of the workpiece. Tighten the clamp to secure the workpiece.

99

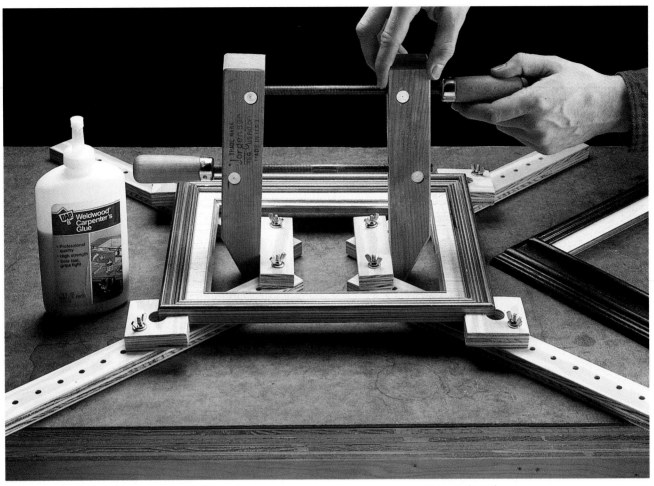

This easy-to-build miter clamp and one handscrew are all you need to make perfect frames.

Build a Four-corner Miter Clamp for Easy Frame-making

This adjustable miter clamp lets you clamp four corners at the same time when building picture frames or cabinet front frames. The miter clamp is built from scrap pieces of ¾" plywood, and is tightened with a single handscrew or bar clamp. The miter clamp adjusts to fit a variety of frame sizes.

For very large or very small frames, build additional miter clamps scaled to fit the frames.

Everything You Need:

Tools: pencil, framing square, jig saw, drill, bits (¼" twist, ¾" spade), handscrew or bar clamp.

Materials: scrap ¾" plywood, eight ¼" × 2" machine screws with washers and wing nuts.

Lumber Cutting List

Key	Pieces	Size and description
A	4	¾" clamp arms, 1½" × 16"
B	2	¾" cross bars, 1½" × 5"
C	4	¾" corner blocks, 2½" square

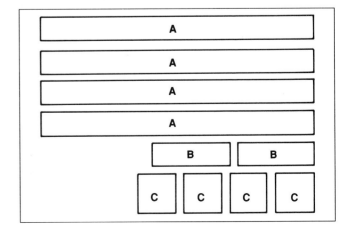

How to Build a Four-corner Miter Clamp

1 Draw a line lengthwise down the center of each miter clamp arm (A), using a framing square as a guide.

2 Mark locations for drill holes every 1" along the centerline on each arm. Drill a hole through the arm at each mark, using a ¼" bit.

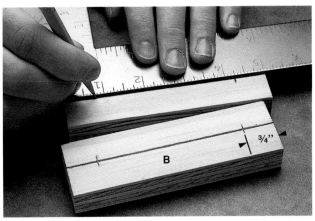

3 Draw a line lengthwise down the center of each cross bar (B). Mark two points on each centerline, ¾" from the ends of the cross bar. Drill holes at each marked point, using a ¼" bit.

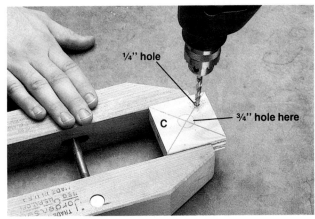

4 Draw a pair of diagonal lines across each corner block (C). On each block, mark a pivot point on one of the diagonal lines, ¾" from one corner. Drill a hole at the pivot point, using a ¼" bit. Drill another hole where diagonal lines intersect, using a ¾" bit.

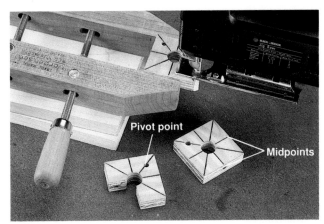

5 Find the midpoint of each side of the corner block, and use these points to mark perpendicular lines across the block. Using the lines as a guide, cut away the corner that is opposite from the pivot point.

6 Assemble the four-corner miter clamp by loosely joining the parts with machine screws, washers, and wing nuts. Use the miter clamp as shown on the opposite page.

Instant Work Surface

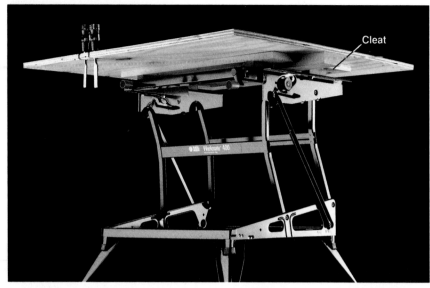

Cleat

A clamping workbench, like the Workmate® work center, is convenient, portable, and easy to store. You can expand the working surface of a portable workbench by attaching a 4 ft. × 4 ft. piece of plywood to a 2 × 4 cleat. Lay the plywood on the work center, and clamp the cleat between the workbench jaws. Drill holes along the edge of the work surface to hold screwdrivers, chisels, and other small tools.

Versatile Accessory Clamps

Make clamping more convenient by using portable workbench accessories, such as bench stops (A), horizontal clamps (B), and hold-down clamps (C). To use these accessories with a standard workbench, drill mounting holes in the workbench top.

Put Bench Tools on a Pedestal

Mount small bench tools, like a bench grinder, band saw, or router table, on a portable workbench for safe and easy use. Attach the tool to a ¾" plywood pedestal, then place the tool on the workbench and clamp the pedestal between bench stops.

Grip in Groove

Clamp cylindrical workpieces, like metal pipes, between the jaws of the portable workbench. The edges of the jaws are grooved to help hold cylindrical objects more securely.

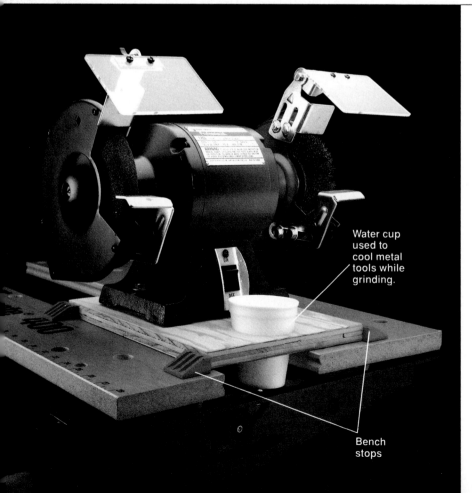

Water cup used to cool metal tools while grinding.

Bench stops

Easy Door Clamp

To clamp a door on edge when planing an edge or routing hinge mortises, position the door next to a portable workbench and clamp the end of the door in the workbench jaws.

Short-Story

Make a "shorty" work station by retracting the lower legs on the workbench. Retracting the legs brings large workpieces down to a comfortable working height.

Refurbish Your Portable Workbench

Refurbish a portable workbench by replacing the damaged surface material with a new top cut from ¾" high-density particleboard or solid-core plywood. Use the old top as a template for making cutouts in the new workbench top, and reuse the old hardware. Use a router to cut grooves on the inside edge of each top piece for holding cylindrical objects.

Clamp Down on It

Large, flat workpieces can be clamped by rotating the movable jaw to a vertical position. Clamping in this position works well when routing edges on a workpiece.

Adhesive Type	Characteristics	Uses
White glue	**Strength:** moderate; rigid bond **Drying time:** several hours **Resistance to heat:** poor **Resistance to moisture:** poor **Hazards:** none **Cleanup/solvent:** soap and water	**Porous surfaces:** Wood (indoors) Paper Cloth
Yellow carpenter's glue	**Strength:** moderate to good; rigid bond **Drying time:** several hours; faster than white glue **Resistance to heat:** moderate **Resistance to moisture:** moderate **Hazards:** none **Cleanup/solvent:** soap and water	**Porous surfaces:** Wood (indoors) Paper Cloth
Two-part epoxy	**Strength:** excellent; strongest of all adhesives **Drying time:** varies, depending on manufacturer **Resistance to heat:** excellent **Resistance to moisture:** excellent **Hazards:** fumes are toxic and flammable **Cleanup/solvent:** acetone will dissolve some types	**Smooth & porous surfaces:** Wood (indoors & outdoors) Metal Masonry Glass Fiberglass
Hot glue	**Strength:** depends on type **Drying time:** less than 60 seconds **Resistance to heat:** fair **Resistance to moisture:** good **Hazards:** hot glue can cause burns **Cleanup/solvent:** heat will loosen bond	**Smooth & porous surfaces:** Glass Plastics Wood
Cyanoacrylate (instant) glue	**Strength:** excellent, but with little flexibility **Drying time:** a few seconds **Resistance to heat:** excellent **Resistance to moisture:** excellent **Hazards:** can bond skin instantly; toxic, flammable **Cleanup/solvent:** acetone	**Smooth surfaces:** Glass Ceramics Plastics Metal
Latex acrylic panel adhesive	**Strength:** good to excellent; very durable **Drying time:** 24 hours **Resistance to heat:** good **Resistance to moisture:** excellent **Hazards:** may irritate skin and eyes **Cleanup/solvent:** soap and water (while still wet)	**Porous surfaces:** Framing lumber Plywood and paneling Wallboard Foam panels Masonry
Water-base contact cement	**Strength:** good **Drying time:** bonds instantly; dries fully in 30 minutes **Resistance to heat:** excellent **Resistance to moisture:** good **Hazards:** may irritate skin and eyes **Cleanup/solvent:** soap and water (while still wet)	**Porous surfaces:** Plastic laminates Plywood Flooring Cloth
Silicone sealant	**Strength:** fair to good; very flexible bond **Drying time:** 24 hours **Resistance to heat:** good **Resistance to moisture:** excellent **Hazards:** may irritate skin and eyes **Cleanup/solvent:** acetone	**Smooth & porous surfaces:** Wood Porcelain Fiberglass Plastics Glass

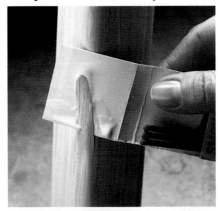

Easy Fix for Wood Splinters

To apply glue to a wood splinter without breaking it off, use a matchbook cover. Apply a small amount of yellow carpenter's glue to the matchbook cover, then slide it under the wood sliver to coat it with glue. Wipe away excess glue with a damp cloth, then cover the splinter with wax paper or a scrap of rubber. Hold the splinter in place overnight with a wood block and C-clamp.

Spread Yourself Thin

For strong wood joints, the surfaces need a thin, even coating of glue. Make your own glue applicator from a thin strip of wood, a craft stick, a clothespin with a short piece of rope, or an old toothbrush.

Stick with Safe Glues

If you have a choice between water-based (latex) adhesives and solvent-based adhesives, always choose the latex products. Latex adhesives are less toxic than solvent-based products, are not flammable, and do not emit harmful vapors. Adhesives now available in latex form include contact cements, panel adhesives, and sealants. Identify latex products by looking for the words "water cleanup" or "latex" printed on their labels.

Avoid Sticky Situations

Glue seeping from wood joints can bond to a pipe clamp or C-clamp. Prevent this by placing wax paper between the clamp and the workpiece.

Ready-to-go Glue

Store glue bottles upside down so the glue is ready to pour whenever it is needed. Make a glue bottle holder by drilling holes in a scrap 1 × 4 and attaching it to a wall or a pegboard storage panel.

Furniture Fix

Regluing a loose furniture joint is difficult if the joint is dirty or caked with old glue and varnish. Before regluing, wash the joint with warm vinegar to remove caked-on glue. Rinse with clear water, and let the wood dry completely before gluing with yellow carpenter's glue.

Glue Gauge

When using epoxy adhesive, it is difficult to tell when it is dry. At the same time you apply adhesive to a workpiece, make a glue gauge by applying a small amount of epoxy to a piece of scrap wood. When the epoxy sample is dry, so is the workpiece.

How to Reglue Loose Veneer

1 Use a putty knife to gently pry up the edge of the loose veneer. Carefully scrape away the old glue.

2 Apply a thin coat of yellow carpenter's glue to the surfaces, using a cotton swab or craft stick. Press the veneer in place, and wipe away any excess carpenter's glue with a damp cloth.

3 Cover the glued area with wax paper or a scrap of rubber, and clamp it with a block of wood and a C-clamp. Let the glue dry overnight.

Getting out of a Bind

If you have trouble taking wood joints apart to repair them, try using a chemical solvent. Mineral spirits dissolve some adhesives, but the fumes are toxic and flammable. Acetone is a powerful solvent that dissolves most adhesives, but its fumes are highly toxic and very flammable. **Use these products only in well-ventilated areas.**

Nontoxic Remover for Tile Adhesive

Chemical solvents for removing tile adhesives are messy, toxic, and flammable. Instead of using chemical solvents, you may be able to use a heat gun to soften adhesives. Apply heat carefully so that the adhesive is softened but not scorched. Use a wide-blade wallboard knife to scrape away the adhesive. If you suspect that your tiles or tile adhesive contain asbestos, contact an asbestos-removal professional to have the tiles removed.

Remove Dried Glue with a Chisel

Carpenter's glue is nearly invisible when it dries — until you stain the wood (inset). To prevent streaks, remove dried glue before you start finishing, using a sharp chisel that has the corners rounded off to prevent gouging the wood. Hold the chisel with the bevel side down when scraping away dried glue.

Glue Trowel

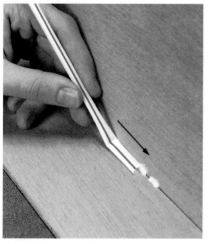

Remove excess glue from inside corners while it is still wet, using a drinking straw. Crease the straw near the tip and push it along the corner to remove the excess glue.

Less Mess

Cover your work surface with wax paper before setting a glued workpiece on it. The wax paper prevents seeping glue from bonding to the work surface.

Great Guns for Good Gluing

Use a hot glue gun instead of white household glue or yellow carpenter's glue to bond smooth surfaces, like plastic or glass. Most hot glues set up in less than 1 minute, so no clamping is required. The cordless hot glue gun shown above uses a small, replaceable butane fuel cartridge to heat the glue.

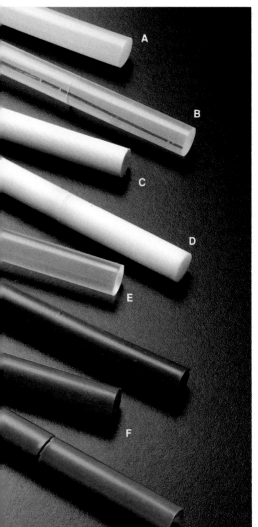

Walk Softly & Carry Several Sticks

Adhesive sticks for hot glue guns are available in several types for specialty uses.

(A) General-purpose adhesive dries clear, and is good for general bonding.

(B) Fast-drying adhesive, identified by a stripe, dries in 30 seconds or less.

(C) Wood-glue adhesive bonds well with wood fibers. It dries to an opaque cream color.

(D) Caulk/sealer adhesive is made to withstand changes in temperature and moisture, and can be used to weatherproof doors and windows.

(E) Ceramic/glass adhesive dries very quickly, and is invisible when dry.

(F) Craft adhesive comes in decorative colors to enhance your projects.

Nifty Nozzles

A needle nozzle is ideal for injecting glue into tight areas, and for small craft projects.

A wide spreader nozzle works well when gluing large surfaces or when filling large gaps with caulk-type adhesive.

Hot Caulker/Sealer

Fill small cracks around doors and windows using a hot glue gun loaded with caulk/sealer sticks. Hot glue guns work well in areas too small for a conventional glue gun, and in cool conditions where ordinary caulks become thick and difficult to apply.

Hot Glue Warm-up

Because hot glues dry very quickly, you may have trouble gluing large surfaces that require a lot of glue. Delay the drying time slightly by warming the workpiece surfaces with a heat gun before applying the adhesive. Apply the adhesive quickly, using a wide spreader nozzle (page opposite), and position the workpieces immediately.

Glue Gun Rack

Hot glue guns are useful tools, but they can be messy; and the hot metal tips can cause burns if the gun is not handled carefully.

The easy-to-make glue gun rack shown here works better than the built-in wire stands found on some glue guns. It provides a broad base to keep the hot glue gun from tipping over, and includes a drip-catcher.

The glue gun rack is built from a 4" × 8" wooden base (A), a 1" × 3" support block (B), a metal spring clip (C), and a metal jar lid (D). Join all the pieces together with hot glue.

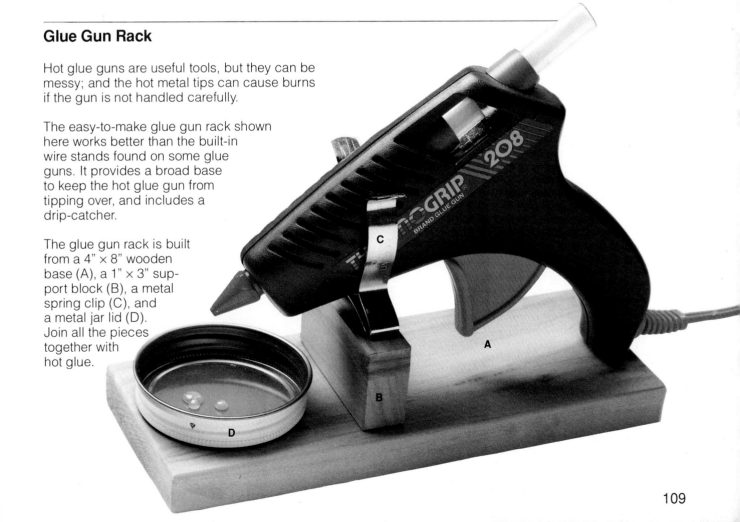

All in a Flap

Make your own flap sander for smoothing wood contours, using a 6" length of ⅜" wooden dowel and a 1" strip of cloth-backed sandpaper, such as that used for sanding belts. To make the flap sander, cut a 1" slot down the center of the dowel. Hot-glue the strip of cloth-backed sandpaper into the slot. Facing the slotted end of the dowel, wrap the sandpaper strip around the dowel in a clockwise direction. Attach the flap sander to a power drill.

Sanding Belt Cleaner

Extend the life of sanding belts by cleaning them with an old tennis shoe that has a natural rubber sole. Turn the sander on and press the tennis shoe against the belt for a few seconds. Wood dust trapped between the abrasives on the sanding belt will cling to the rubber sole of the shoe.

Sanding Extension

Make a sanding extension arm by taping sandpaper around the head of a sponge mop. The extension arm works well for sanding walls before painting, or for smoothing hard-to-reach wallboard joints.

Extra Pair of Hands

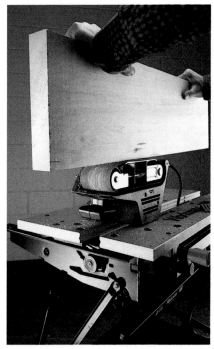

With some jobs, it is easier to clamp a power tool in place rather than the workpiece. The Work-mate® portable work station works well for this purpose. Clamp the tool securely, but do not over-tighten, or the tool casing may bend or crack.

Get a Handle on Your Sanding

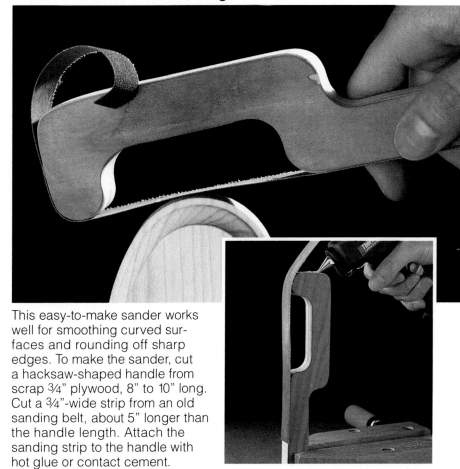

This easy-to-make sander works well for smoothing curved sur-faces and rounding off sharp edges. To make the sander, cut a hacksaw-shaped handle from scrap ¾" plywood, 8" to 10" long. Cut a ¾"-wide strip from an old sanding belt, about 5" longer than the handle length. Attach the sanding strip to the handle with hot glue or contact cement.

Sandwich Sanding

When using a power sander to smooth the edge of a board, clamp it between two pieces of scrap lumber to prevent the power sander from wobbling and rounding off the edges.

Emery Sanders

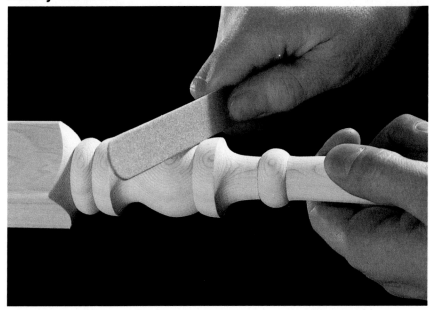

Use emery boards to sand tight areas where a sanding block or power sander will not fit. Emery boards work well on decorative spindles and for smoothing tight corners before finishing.

Sandpaper Saw

Attach an old hacksaw blade to the edge of your workbench with screws, and use it as a convenient sandpaper cutter.

Stack the Deck

Wrap a piece of fine-grit sandpaper around an old deck of playing cards to make a contour sander that sands low points without flattening high points. The deck of cards shapes itself to the contours of the workpiece for quick and accurate sanding.

Just Your Size

Make a template to save time when cutting sandpaper sheets for a power sander. To make the template, cut a piece of ¾" lumber to match the sandpaper size your sander requires. Cut the edges of the template at a sharp-angled bevel to provide a cutting edge for tearing the paper.

Screen Sander

Wrap a piece of leftover window screening around a scrap 2 × 4 and staple it in place to make a good block sander for smoothing wallboard joints.

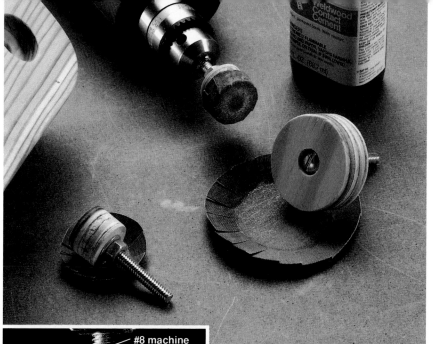

Hose It Down

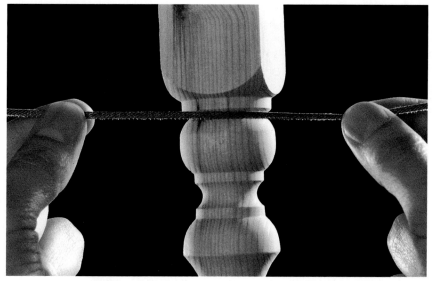

Disc-o Sander

Sand hard-to-reach recesses by making a custom-sized disc sander. Cut a small circle of finish plywood, and drill a countersunk hole through the center. Attach a machine screw to the plywood with a washer, lock washer, and nut. Attach the screw to the drill chuck. Cut a sandpaper disc and attach it the plywood circle with contact cement. To sand both the sides and bottom of a recess, cut the sandpaper disc larger than the plywood (above), then make slits in the edges and fold the sandpaper up around the plywood.

#8 machine screw

Nut

Lock washer

¼" hole

Washer

½" counterbore

Contact cement

(Shown cut away)

Wrap a piece of sandpaper around a short length of old garden hose to make a sander for smoothing curves. If you wish, use hot glue to attach the sandpaper.

Hold It Right There

When sanding a small, flat workpiece, hold it in place by laying it on a piece of carpet padding or sandpaper. To keep the padding or sandpaper from slipping, hot-glue it to the work surface.

In the Groove

Sand hard-to-reach crevices in decorative spindles and millwork pieces with narrow strips cut from cloth-backed sanding belts.

The One That Gets Really Used

Keep old phone books and catalogs to use as renewable work surfaces for small painting and gluing projects. Tear out dirty pages to provide a clean work surface for the next job.

Testing One, Two, Three

Keep scraps of wood on hand for testing the color of wood stains and finishing oils. For an accurate test, the wood scrap should be the same type of wood as the workpiece, and should have a similar grain pattern.

Glue-stain Remover

Remove glue stains with a solution of oxalic acid. Wearing rubber gloves, mix 1 part acid to 12 parts water. Moisten a cloth in the solution and rub the stain until gone. Before applying finish or paint, clean workpiece with a solution of equal parts of water and vinegar to neutralize the acid.

Tacky Cloth for Fine Finishing

Woodworking projects requiring two or more coats of varnish or stain can be ruined if dust settles on the workpiece between coats. Before applying each new coat, wipe the workpiece with a tack cloth. Make your own tack cloth by moistening a lint-free cloth with a mixture of equal parts of turpentine and oil-based varnish. Store homemade tack rags in a coffee can or other airtight container.

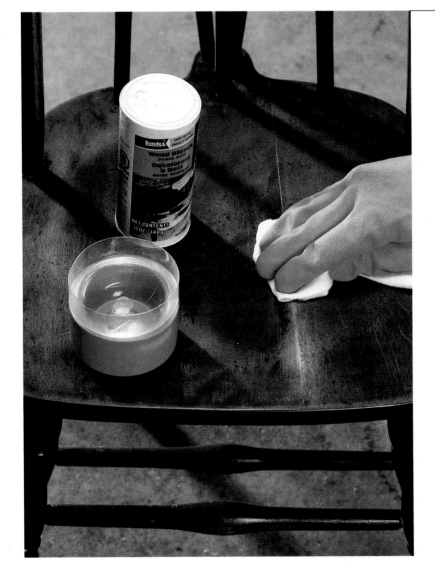

Steamy Story

Hammer marks and other small dents in wood can be repaired with steam. Dampen a small scrap of cloth, and place the cloth over the dent (A). Apply heat to the cloth with an iron (B). Moisture in the cloth will turn to steam and cause the wood to swell. Sand the spot lightly after the wood dries (C).

Dentil Work

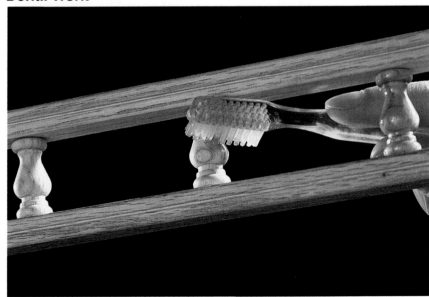

Use an old toothbrush to apply wipe-on stains to hard-to-reach crevices on spindle moldings and other decorative trim pieces.

Child's Play

Small scratches in a paint job or wood finish can be hidden with colored wax from an ordinary crayon. Choose a crayon that matches the color of the workpiece. Heat the crayon slightly with a match or the tip of a hot glue gun, then fill the scratch. Buff the area with a soft cloth after the melted wax dries.

Save a Fine Finish

Remove water spots and rings from wood finishes by scrubbing them gently with a wet cloth and a dab of toothpaste. The toothpaste contains a mild abrasive that will not damage the finish. After removing the stain, buff the area with a dry cloth until the shine returns.

Smear-proof Paint Drying

Painted workpieces can be propped up to dry on wallboard screws driven through small wood blocks. The screw points are very small and sharp, and will not mar a freshly painted surface.

Handling Paint

Protect your hands by making a paint bucket handle from a length of old garden hose. Slice a spiral cut in the hose, then fit the hose over the wire bucket handle.

Breathe Life into It

To prolong the shelf life of latex paint, breathe into the can before sealing it. Breathing into the can adds carbon dioxide, reducing the amount of oxygen that can cause paint to skin over.

Catch Paint Drips

Hot-glue a paper plate to the bottom of a paint can to catch stray paint drips.

Paint-stripping Knife

When stripping paint from decorative moldings, make your own custom stripping tool from an old wallboard knife with a flexible blade. Grind the tool with a bench grinder or file so it fits the contours of the molding. Do not leave any sharp corners that can gouge the wood.

Reduce Paint Cleanup

Drip Drop Stop

Here are two more easy ways to prevent paint drips. Use an old coffee can and plastic lid to hold paint. Cut a hole in the center of the plastic lid, and use it to wipe excess paint from your brush. Paint drips go into the can, not down the sides. Cut the top off a narrow plastic glue bottle and tape it to the side of the can to use as a convenient paint brush holster.

Reduce cleanup time by lining roller trays with plastic garbage bags. Place a wire painting screen, available at home centers, over the plastic to prevent the plastic from wrinkling and clinging to the roller.

The Bottom Line

Take Your Lumps

Paint the bottom edges of doors easily without removing them by using a scrap of carpet coated with paint. Painting the bottom of doors seals the end grain, preventing the wood from absorbing moisture.

Paint that has been stored for a long time can get lumpy. To guarantee a smooth paint finish, first mix the paint thoroughly, then strain it through an old nylon stocking, a piece of window screening, or cheesecloth placed over the mouth of a coffee can.

Workshop Cleanup
& Recycling

- Cleanup
- Recycling Tips
- Using Leftovers

Keep your workshop free of sawdust and waste materials. In a cluttered, dirty workshop you are more likely to have accidents, misplace tools, spoil expensive materials, and ruin workpieces. This concluding chapter includes dozens of tips to help make workshop cleanup faster and easier.

An average workshop produces nearly 30 pounds of sawdust each year. If sawdust builds up, it can clog tool motors and gears, create a workshop fire hazard, and enter the home ventilation system to spread throughout the house. Instead of sweeping, use a heavy-duty shop vacuum to remove sawdust and dirt. Sweeping increases levels of airborne dust.

Paints, varnishes, cleaning solutions, solvents, and many other products used in the workshop are toxic and flammable. This section presents many helpful tips for disposing of these products.

Finally, you will find a special section showing you how to turn throwaway household items into valuable workshop aids. By making use of these "leftovers," you can save time and money while cutting down on household trash.

Portable Dust Filter

Trap dust by taping a furnace filter to the intake side of a window fan. Place the fan next to your work area to clean dust from the air when sanding or sawing. When the filter becomes dirty, vacuum it clean and reuse it.

Dust Dumpster

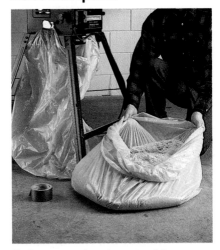

Collect sawdust by attaching a garbage bag to the bottom of your table saw with duct tape.

Winning the War against Dust

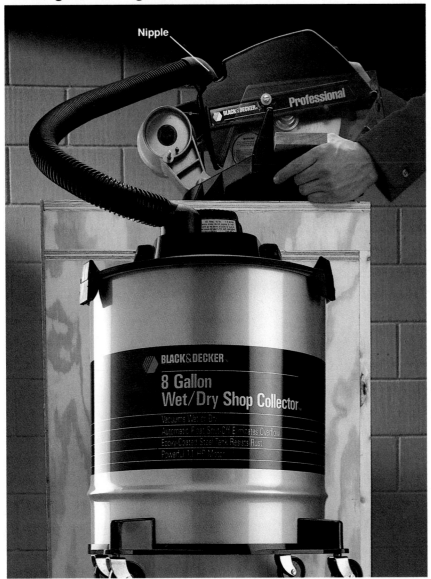

Some stationary tools, such as power miter saws and radial arm saws, have blade guard nipples that can be attached directly to a shop vacuum hose. Before using the saw, turn on the vacuum to remove the sawdust as you work.

Handy Hand Cleaner

Hands soiled with oil or oil-based paints and stains can be cleaned with ordinary salad oil. Never use kerosene, mineral spirits, or other solvents to wash skin, because these hazardous materials are skin irritants and can be absorbed by the body.

Breathe Deeply

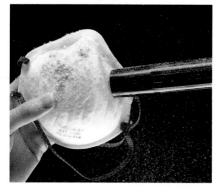

Particle filter masks usually can be cleaned with a shop vacuum and reused, but they should be thrown away when they become badly soiled. Change dirty particle filters on a respirator mask (page 8) frequently.

Confine the Cleanup

Hang sheets of plastic around your work area to confine the dust when sawing or sanding. Turn off the heating and air-conditioning system to prevent it from carrying fine sawdust throughout the house.

Quick & Clean

Hard-to-reach areas are difficult to clean with standard shop vacuum attachments. Make a powerful, flexible mini vacuum attachment, using a plastic plumbing tube and transition fittings, available at plumbing supply stores. Whenever it is needed, connect the attachment to your shop vacuum to clean crevices and tight areas, like the spaces around a table saw motor.

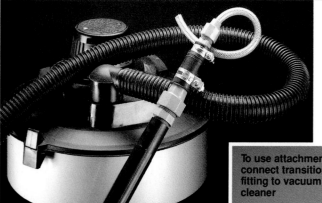

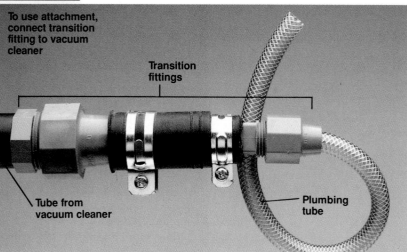

To use attachment, connect transition fitting to vacuum cleaner

Transition fittings

Tube from vacuum cleaner

Plumbing tube

Paint Brush Cleanup

Conserve on paint solvents, such as mineral spirits and liquid brush cleaners, by using narrow plastic bottles to clean your paint brushes. A small container requires a smaller volume of solvent to cover the bristles.

Keep Your Spirits Up

Place used mineral spirits in a sealed container until solid paint sediments settle out. Pour off the clear solvent for later use, then set the residue outdoors in a protected location where children and pets cannot reach it. Let the residue dry completely, then throw it away with household trash.

Memory Minder

Check labels before disposing of a product, and never pour hazardous liquids into a drain system. Make a hazardous waste reminder list and post it above your utility sink. Products rated as environmental hazards by the U.S. Environmental Protection Agency will carry one or more of the following terms: **Danger! Toxic, Harmful to Animals and Humans, Harmful Vapors, Poison, Flammable, Combustible, Corrosive, Explosive.**

Paint Disposal

To get rid of small amounts of unwanted paint, remove the lids and set the cans outdoors in a protected area where children and pets cannot reach them. Let the paint dry completely before throwing it away. Sand or sawdust can be added to absorb paint and speed up drying.

Clean Clothes

Wash shop clothing and cloth work gloves frequently. Launder shop clothing separately from other household laundry, because dust and grime from treated lumber and other products may leave a skin-irritating residue, even after washing.

Don't Bury Your Troubles

Household batteries and rechargeable tool batteries contain heavy metals, such as lead, cadmium, mercury, and zinc. If buried in a landfill, these toxic metals leach into the water supply, causing public health problems. Never throw batteries away with household trash. Check the Yellow Pages under "Recycling Services" for companies that handle these materials.

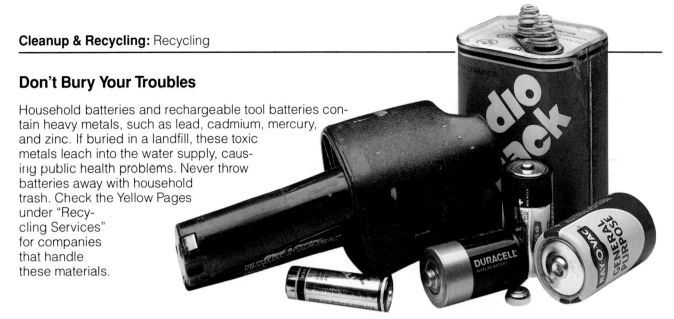

That'll Teach You

Donate old power tools to vocational education centers for use in training classes. Your tool donations may be tax deductible.

Recycle Most Metals

Recycling companies in your area may buy or collect many types of scrap metal, including steel, iron, lead, and copper from electrical wiring and plumbing pipes.

Save Your Leftovers

Combine partial cans of leftover paint in one container to create a usable amount of paint for another project. Use paints that have similar colors so that the resulting tint is pleasing to the eye. Do not mix latex with solvent-based paints. You also can give leftover paint to church groups and civic organizations, as long as the original product labels are not removed.

Turn Shop Sawdust into Garden Gold

Sawdust and shavings from pine and oak lumber can be composted to form a nutritious mulch for gardens, shrubs, and trees. The best mulches are formed by mixing the sawdust and shavings with other lawn compost, like leaves and grass clippings. Mulch with a high percentage of pine sawdust is excellent for acid-loving plants, like evergreen shrubs and azaleas, but may be too acidic for vegetable gardens unless you also add nitrogen fertilizer to the compost. Never compost sawdust from pressure-treated lumber, plywood, or particleboard, which contain hazardous additives.

Cedar Scenter

Absorb Mistakes

Keep a few coffee cans full of dry sawdust on hand for absorbing spilled liquids in the shop. Sawdust also works well to prevent slipping on icy winter sidewalks. Unlike chemical deicers, sawdust will not harm lawns or shrubs.

Place shavings from aromatic cedar into the toe of an old nylon stocking. Tie off the toe, cut away the excess material, and use the pouch to scent a dresser drawer or closet.

High & Dry Lumber Storage

Use old auto tires to create a pallet for stacking plywood and lumber. A tire pallet provides even support so that sheets do not bend, and keeps wood away from floor-level moisture that can cause wood to rot.

Using Leftovers

Dozens of leftover household items can find creative new life in the hands of an imaginative do-it-yourselfer. Refer to the page listings under the following photos for additional ways to turn household trash into workshop treasure.

Toothbrushes: saw blade cleaner (page 60), glue applicator (105), stain applicator (115).

Tennis balls: soft-headed mallet (page 41), chisel protector (46), plier clamps (94), clamp pads (97).

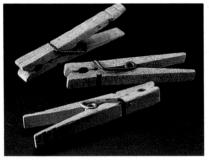

Clothespins: vise clamps (page 93), glue applicator (105).

Old telephone books & catalogs: renewable work surface (page 114).

Hacksaw blades: mini hacksaw (page 53), sandpaper cutter (112).

Plastic oil containers: tool cord organizer (page 23).

Electrical wire nuts: replacement caps for glue and caulk (page 22).

Garden hose: saw blade guard (page 44), hand sander (113), bucket handle (116).

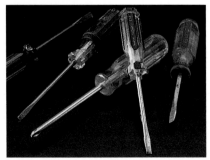

Tools: specialty tools (pages 50 to 51), woodworking mallet (52), paint scraper (53), glue remover (107), paint-stripping knife (116).

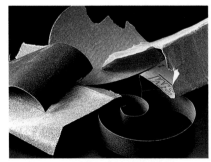

Sandpaper & emery boards: pencil sharpener (page 52), vise pads (95), sanding extension (110) , crevice sander (111, 113).

Plastic containers & caps: rag storage (page 20), cord carrier (26), clamp pads (94), paint brush holder (117), brush cleaner (121).

Window screening: light fixture protector (page 8), block sander (112), paint strainer (117).

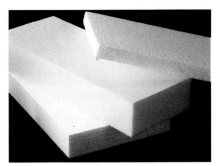

Rigid foam: router bit holder (page 26), blade guard (44), saw blade holder (76).

Paint & painting solvents: solvent saver (page 121), using leftover paint (122).

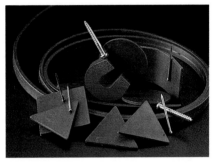

Magnets: tool holders (pages 22, 52), magnetic screwdriver (53).

Pipes: clamps (pages 96 to 99), recycling (122).

Battery jumper cables: spring clamps (page 93).

Coffee cans: rag storage (page 114), paint holder (117), sawdust holder (123).

Inner tubes: pads for tool legs (page 14), band clamps (92, 99), pliers spring clamp (93).

Nylon stockings: tourniquet clamp (page 94), paint strainer (117), cedar sachet (123).

Carpet & padding: tool leg pads (pages 14, 72), car roof scratch guard (16), rust preventer (39), painting pad for door edges (117).

Scrap wood: saw blade caddy (page 20), under-stairs storage shelf (23), storage boxes (25), handsaw guide (45), circular saw straightedge guide (56), crosscut guide for circular saws (57), support stand for table saws (66), pads for vise jaws (95), four-corner miter clamp (100), strip sander (111).

Index

For Product Information:

If you have difficulty finding any of the following materials featured in this book, call
the manufacturers and ask for the name of
the nearest sales representative. The representative can direct you to local retailers
that stock the product you are looking for.

Anti-fatigue mats (page 7)
Durable Mat Company,
  telephone: 1-800-537-1603.
Electronic levels (page 84)
Wedge Innovations,
  telephone: 1-800-SMARTLEVEL.
Soundproofing products (pages 14-15)
Homasote Company (440® board),
  telephone: 1-800-257-9491.
Armstrong World Industries (acoustical tile),
  telephone: 1-800-233-3823.
Sonic measuring tools (page 85)
Cooper Tools (Lufkin® ultrasonic tool),
  telephone: 919-362-7510.
Sonin Inc. (ultrasonic measuring tool),
  telephone: 1-800-223-7511.

Cy DeCosse Incorporated offers Black
& Decker® tools at special subscriber
discounts. For information write:

Black & Decker Tools
5900 Green Oak Drive
Minnetonka, MN 55343